For D[illegible]
I a[illegible]
book. Keep smiling :)
God Bless
Love
Mary

Mary [illegible]

my mom died and I'm okay

overcoming the pain of living
with the dying

by
mary elizabeth keilman

#13 of 250 1st shipment 8/24/2007

AuthorHouse™
1663 Liberty Drive, Suite 200
Bloomington, IN 47403
www.authorhouse.com
Phone: 1-800-839-8640

First published by AuthorHouse 7/27/2007

ISBN: 978-1-4343-1716-2 (sc)

Library of Congress Control Number: 2007904728

Printed in the United States of America
Bloomington, Indiana

This book is printed on acid-free paper.

For Mom, Dad and my three sisters. And for Lisa... who lived on the second floor...and often smiled even when she was in pain. It was nothing short of a gift that God let me meet you before he called you home.

Table of Contents

Prologue

My mom went to a friend's wake in April 2001 and brought this poem for me to keep in a safe place. For months I carried it in my purse; then I decided to put it in a desk drawer for safe keeping. It is the one she wants when she dies.

God saw her getting tired,
And a cure was not to be
So he put his arms around her
And whispered, "Come with me."

With tearful hearts we watched her
Suffer, and saw her fade away.
Although we loved her dearly,
We could not make her stay.

A golden heart stopped beating.
Hard working hands to rest.
God broke our hearts to prove to us,
He only takes the best.

My fiancé, Al, the second youngest of twelve, grew up on a dairy farm in northwest Indiana. I had never met anyone who came from a family of twelve before, let alone imagined I would marry into one.

"My sister Ginny loves to talk," Al said as we waited for the elevator in her apartment building. We would pick her up from her senior apartment located in the southwest suburbs of Chicago on our way to visit his family in Indiana. Al is a man of his word. Ginny started talking from the minute she greeted us at the door, and never stopped until we arrived at our destination about an hour and a half later. I came to enjoy her as we got to know one another. I am several years younger than Al, and she was several years older, hence there was a considerable age difference between me and my future sister-in-law. But we got along just fine. We both had a good sense of humor, and she loved it when I teased her.

One time as we arrived at a family reunion she realized she forgot to bring the two heads of lettuce for the salad she had prepared. "What the hell am I going to do with two heads of lettuce at my apartment?!" she thought out loud. Al waited in the car as Ginny and I went into the grocery store to replace the forgotten lettuce. As she put the lettuce and a couple of bananas on the belt, I looked at the teenaged girl behind the register and said, "I got that."

"No, way," Ginny protested, "you're not paying for my lettuce!"

"For Pete's sake, Ginny, give me a break! It's just a couple of dollars."

"Oh, no you're not!" she said as she attempted to push me aside with her little body, her hands busy digging around in her purse. I am several inches taller than Ginny and was not budging. I already had my arm outstretched, money in hand.

"Don't you take her money!" Ginny told the cashier as she offered her a five dollar bill.

"Don't take *her* money," I said and winked. The cashier looked at the two of us, not sure if we were kidding around or fighting. We went back and forth like that until Ginny looked at the cashier and said, "Can you believe this is my future sister-in-law?" Now, remember, there were about forty years separating us. The girl gave her a funny look. I did not miss a beat.

"Grandma! Will you please stop telling people that?" I said as I looked at the young girl and circled my pointer finger close to my head to indicate her insanity.

Ginny was flustered. "Why, you little...!"

Then I paid the lady.

We were busting with laughter as we got into the car. Ginny told Al all about it, and the look on the girl's face. Ginny always pretended that she was irritated with our teasing, but she loved the attention.

Over the next couple of years Ginny's health deteriorated, and she was in and out of the hospital a few times. We would visit her when our busy schedule allowed. The last time I talked with her on the phone I could barely understand her slurred speech. One Wednesday in April 2003 Al and I took the day off to visit Ginny at the hospital. She was too sick to live independently and would have to give up her apartment in Tinley Park. The next step was a nursing home; that was the last place she wanted to go.

Ginny ate that day, which was good I suppose because she had not been eating very much lately. Although she was confused, she knew us and was awake most of the day, and we were able to visit with her. As we left, Al and I talked about how our next visit would be at the nursing home. She passed away the next day. *There would be no pictures of Ginny dancing at her little brother's wedding.*

I was introduced to Wally during the early stages of my "friendship" with Al. Wally married Al's older sister Rudie when Al was just a boy. They would go hunting or fishing, and as the years progressed, Wally, in spite of a short temper, became more like a father figure to Al and some of the other younger siblings. By the time I met him his hair was snow white, but I could picture him as a much younger man. He had one of those perfect crew cuts, nice and even across the top. He was a big guy who would say what he thought, but he had a big heart.

The first time I met Wally, he and Rudie came to visit with another one of the brothers and his wife. At the time Al and I lived across the street from each other. We gathered at Al's for a barbecue, and as I stood working at the kitchen sink, I looked out the window towards the backyard where the guys had gathered around the grill. Wally caught my eye and smiled, put his hand up and moved his fat fingers in a wave. This was encouraging to me…think about it, here I was, meeting bits and pieces of a very large family. Al was recently divorced, and I was not sure how the family would accept the idea of a new girlfriend. But we had a great time getting acquainted that weekend, and often visited Wally and Rudie and many others over the next couple of years.

Well, Wally got sick. I guess he was sick for a long time; he used oxygen the whole time I knew him. His health worsened and eventually there was a need for hospice care. That went on for a grueling eighteen months. We all knew he was dying. After each visit I saw the pain in Al's eyes and realized he knew this could be the last time he would see his Wally.

The very day after Ginny passed away, we received another phone call from the family. Wally had died. He suffered no more. Now the family would prepare for two funerals instead of one.

The poem my mother chose is a popular one, and when it was read at Ginny's funeral, I could not contain my emotions. We were huddled at the cemetery. As I sobbed, Al and one of my future sisters-in-law stood strong on either side of me and held me tight around the waist. I mourned for these nice people, who would become my extended family. I cried when we sang "How Great Thou Art" at the wake the night before. I cried for Ginny and for Wally and for all of Al's family for their losses. And I cried at the foreboding that all of these rituals would be repeated at my own mother's funeral, and it would be sooner rather than later.

Here is my story.

Much of the content spilled out of my soul

as I struggled my way through it.

CHAPTER ONE

Brief History

My mother, Arlene Cable, was in her late forties when she was diagnosed with breast cancer. After enduring a lumpectomy, brutal radiation and chemotherapy treatments (which we thought might kill her), she slowly regained her health and a renewed appreciation for life. What I will tell you is that during her first bout with cancer, I was a junior at Northern Illinois University and made every excuse not to come home. I was either too busy working or studying to make the short one hour trip. There may have been a few parties that I went to as well, but I was not about to tell my mother that, as if she did not already know.

Whether it was subconscious or not, I avoided my sick mother like the plague. No one in our family ever had cancer, not that I knew of anyway. I had no idea how to deal with it. You know the old fight or flight? I chose flight. I came home maybe one weekend in the middle of her grueling chemo schedule only to find her sleeping and sleeping and sleeping. Then when she finally woke up, she asked me why I did not wake her up to give her something to eat and something to drink. How was I to know what to do? I never took care of any sick people before. Better for me to stay away.

Through her treatments she continued to work as a special education teacher. She told me she would lie down to rest during her lunch hour. She was determined to not give up, to maintain normalcy in her life.

As she healed from her surgery and treatments, time moved on. There was the one year scan...cancer free! The two year scan...no cancer! The three year, the four year, and then, the golden five years with no signs of cancer. She beat it!

When I was about twenty-six or twenty-seven I remember sitting on my mother's bed one afternoon as she put laundry away. I am not sure how our conversation led to the topic of her cancer, but I found myself needing to express the regret I had been carrying. Now a little older and a little more mature, I realized how selfish I had been during those college years. I regretted not being there during her surgery, her chemo. I regretted not being there for *any* of it.

"I guess I thought you could die, Mom, and I wasn't going to be around to watch it."

She looked at me with her blue eyes and took in what I was saying.

"I'm sorry," I said with sincerity. All I could think of was all the times she cared for me, mothered me, was scared for me. When I came down with mono at the age of eleven, she gave up a job she loved to stay home and take care of me. In spite of everything she had given, I had been unable to put my selfish emotions aside to help her when she had breast cancer.

"Mary," she said, "in this life people do the best they can. I understood a long time ago that you couldn't handle it. I didn't blame you. So let it go."

"It wasn't right, Mom," I said as one lonely tear streamed down my face.

"I forgive you," she said.

We shared some tears and some hugs, and then we went shopping. Something happened that day; I felt like my mom saw me more as an adult than she had before. We bonded.

She enjoyed a life of fairly good health and remission before the return of cancer about eight years after her initial diagnosis. The breast cancer had returned mostly in her bones, and also in one lung. She required two major surgeries over the course of about four years to replace tumor-infested bone in her right femur and hip. She suffered and survived more chemo, radiation treatments, times of illness, weight loss, etc. than I want to relay here.

I share what I learned on my journey through the dying process with the sincere hope of helping others. I was not there for her the first time. I would not make that mistake again.

Early September 2003

"I can't breathe, Mare...and I just cannot get up into the bed."

I furled my brow and processed what my little mother was saying. We had just returned from going out to breakfast with a group of friends.

The front concrete stoop to my house can be a big step if your legs are short. It never posed a problem for my mom before, but today we had to pull her up to get her into the house. I figured she was just tired and needed a nap. I watched her walk down the hallway to the spare bedroom which was now hers when she came to stay over. A minute later she came back down the hall towards me. Her color was not right; she was too pale.

We sat on the couch together and discussed what to do. If we call 911 they would not take her to the appropriate hospital as I live about fifteen miles from her house. But if we do not call 911 there could be severe consequences. We agreed I should call...and we sat close to each other on the couch...and held hands...and said nice things to each other...and waited for the paramedics.

My dad and mom had met us out for breakfast that morning. Essentially dad was dropping mom off for a couple of days. She would stay at our house to give dad a break from his caregiver duties. Plus my mom had always worked and enjoyed a busy social life until her disease would not allow her to go go go anymore, so being cooped up in the house 24/7 was not the healthiest thing for her either.

The paramedics arrived to find us sitting there together, holding hands. I am not tall at 5'6", but I am seven inches taller than my mother. I can imagine what we looked like, sitting there with anticipation and concern on our faces...the big protective daughter and the little soft-around-the-middle, silver-haired mother.

"Hello," one of the handsome young paramedics said. "How are you today?" he asked with a very pleasant expression on his face.

"Fine, thanks," she replied.

"Can you tell me what's wrong?" he asked, as he looked from my mother to me.

"Well," she said, "I'm having trouble breathing."

"Okay, any medical history we should know about?"

My mom and I turned and looked at each other.

Oh boy, where do we start…?

My mother explained she has a return of breast cancer. I interjected bits and pieces as she briefed these young men on her “medical history.” As the story unfolded, the paramedics’ expressions gradually transformed from pleasant to sympathetic. For they knew that this nice little lady, with whom I was still holding hands, and sitting even closer to now, was dying.

“Okay, well, let’s take a look at your vitals. Would you mind moving over a little?”

“Hmm?” I said.

“Ma’am, we would like to check your mother’s vitals,” he said gently.

“Move it, Mary,” my mother said as she grinned and nudged me.

After an examination the nice men determined my mother did not have to go by ambulance, but should seek medical attention. They gave me permission to transport her to her usual hospital about ten miles away. The drive seemed endless.

I had no idea she would never come back to my house again.

CHAPTER TWO

Hospice, Here We Come

I pulled up to the Emergency Room at Central DuPage Hospital and left mom in the car while I went in to retrieve a wheelchair. The cool September breeze, which gently brushed my face and wisped through my fiery red locks, foreshadowed not only the change of season, but also a very significant change in our lives.

We spent hours in the ER that day. I had summoned my father and some other family members. In their usual jovial manner, my parents kidded with the staff, making a potentially heavy mood lighter. Being that it was Sunday, my mother's oncologist was off, so the ER doctor consulted with him via telephone after reading my mother's file. He flipped the curtain back as he came in to deliver the news, courteously nodding at me and my father. From my mother's perspective he must have appeared taller than he really was by standing at the foot of the bed. She looked expectantly at him.

"Your disease, as you know, has progressed. At this point there is really no other treatment. I spoke with your doctor at length, and he recommended we admit you to the Palliative Care Unit. Our main goal is to keep you as comfortable as possible."

I briefly closed my eyes and shook my head. *What?* I thought, *what do you MEAN there is no more treatment? There is always another treatment.*

I could see his lips moving but only comprehended part of what he said. I turned my attention to my mother, whose expression was far from what I expected. She looked...*content*? After he walked away it all started sinking in. Later I would look up palliative in the dictionary.

I quickly learned palliative care is for people who are dying. It is meant to relieve or sooth symptoms without effecting a cure.

My mother seemed okay. She accepted long ago that eventually it would come to this. *Sorry, ma'am. No more treatments.* She had heard of the Palliative Care Unit; she described it like some sort of hotel where the rooms are large and beautiful and you can have whatever you want. She said the reason why the palliative rooms are located on one of the upper floors is so they can be closer to the angels.

Where does she find her spirit in all of this?

She had been lying on her back on the little ER bed in a partially elevated position for hours. Her body language told me her hip ached. She attempted several times with little success to shift her weight into a different position.

After the doctor left, my mother looked at me and immediately read the desperation on my face. I leaned over the bed and grasped the cold side rails that were meant to protect whomever happened to be its current patient. Nothing could protect my mother now. She was DYING! About eleven and a half years after her initial diagnosis with breast cancer, she was going to DIE and nothing could stop it.

A medical doctor, whom we assumed to be educated (although I do not recall asking for his credentials), just told my mother there is nothing else but "keep her comfortable." You would think this was about me; in my mind I was running like a mental patient through my own emotional junkyard.

She looked into my desperate brown eyes. "Now, Mary..."

"No, Ma, there *has* to be something else," I half-pleaded.

"Oh, Mary," she said with a calm, knowing look on her face. "It's okay, Mare...really."

"But, Mom..." I felt helpless; she remained steady.

I felt almost panicked. I don't want my mom to die... not yet...just a little more time...somebody, please...

"Mary, listen to me. We knew it would come to this. It's okay. We'll be okay."

I was totally in shock, devastated. Looking back I do not know why I was so surprised. She was right; we knew it was coming. I suppose I was in denial. Her oncologist, in conjunction with modern medicine, had graced us with three and a half years of options. There were surgeries, treatments, hormone therapy, etc. There was always something else to do, to try, to keep my mother alive and functioning. My mother's oncologist was a godsend. (If you do not like your doctor, get another one!) He even boosted her blood count so she would have more energy for my wedding day. God bless him.

But now, it seemed, just like that, nope, sorry, there is nothing else we can do. You are going to die, and we cannot keep you from dying anymore; however, we will make every effort to keep you comfortable as you are dying. Any questions?

My mom spent a week or so in palliative care while her doctor coordinated with hospice a transition to home. She was still very alert and able to get around by herself in spite of having difficulty breathing. It seemed to me that she slept a lot.

I did not blame her for feeling apprehensive about going home. After all, the hospital provided a safety net of around-the-clock, professionally trained staff; she worried her progressive need for care might be more than we could handle. I was extremely apprehensive, too, but I was not about to tell her that. I reassured her that the hospice people would provide all the advice and support we needed. I had no idea at that point how true that would be.

We brought her home. Soon after, hospice arrived to deliver equipment and complete the necessary paperwork. As the designated power of attorney for healthcare decisions, I signed the documents for my mom. That was a switch. *She* was always the one who signed forms and was in charge of all of *us*.

She is only 60. She is too young for this. I hate cancer.

I helped my dad and my sister Patty rearrange the living room furniture to make way for a hospice bed. As two young men assembled it, my mother escaped down the hallway and crawled into her own bed. My family and I were going through the motions of setting it all up. There were too many people around, and the commotion was getting to her. She was scared and depressed. Accepting her fate was one thing; facing it now proved a harsh reality.

I was scared, too. What if we could not take care of her? When you agree to hospice care you are not supposed to call 911. *But what if there is an emergency?*

It is amazing what you find yourself doing, without difficulty, when caring for a loved one. You want so badly to do everything just right. With time you realize that some days will be better than others, and no matter what happens you are doing your best, and God knows it.

CHAPTER THREE

Laughter and Pie

September 24, 2003

Mom is not bedridden; however, she sleeps a lot now. She takes morphine maybe once a day to control some pain. We keep a medication log in the kitchen to track her meds. Morphine is a great invention in that it also slows her breathing, which is helpful because her pulmonary arteries are not getting enough oxygen due to tumors and radiation damage.

The other day she told me she is surprised at how much she can sleep. Her little body is too weak to do much else. She is frustrated, depressed.

I said, "Well, Mom, I never heard anyone say anything good about end-stage cancer." She pierced her lips and nodded slowly in agreement.

Somehow we keep our sense of humor. Yesterday, while Patty and I were at my parents' house, we found ourselves thinking of different ways to refer to dying. We sat at our mother's side as she rested comfortably in the hospice bed. With her *undying* sense of humor, she encouraged our silliness. Through all of the stress we needed a little comic relief. We came up with a variety of expressions including: "passed away," "died," "crossed over," "crossed the river," "went beyond," "permanently departed," "left this world as we know it," "ascended to heaven," "now walks with Jesus," "turned into an angel," "now lives with us only in spirit," and "has left the building."

"How about 'checked out'," I added.

To which Patty replied, "'croaked'...'kicked the bucket'!"

"'*She's a goner'!*" my mom exclaimed as we burst into laughter.

I know it is morbid, but the laughter must be healthy. We have had four years to think about our mother dying. We need an emotional release other than crying once in a while. My mother often used laughter as the best medicine; why shouldn't we?

One of the best things about dying is you may have whatever you want. Since my mother's diabetes is no longer anyone's concern, she may eat whatever she wants whenever she wants. This includes pie.

There is no time for homemade pies, so we let *Sara Lee* prepare the pies for us, and then we buy them from the frozen foods department at the grocery store. Even dad can bake those.

It is funny. I always connected the smell of pies baking with the holidays. Now we savor the smell every third day or so. Pie is also a great way for me to forget about my own emotions (remember the junkyard?) for a few minutes.

"Honey, are you hungry? Do you want some dinner?" my father will ask her.

After much contemplation on her sweet little face, mom will say, "You got any pie?"

His face brightens as he offers the different flavors of the day. At a time when he is so helpless, this is one way he can still please his sweetheart.

She has no desire for meat of any kind or anything containing tomatoes, such as spaghetti. She cannot stand the smell of pizza. Her body does not produce enough saliva to chew and swallow many foods, especially dry things like crackers. This is normal for a dying person. The dying body is more comfortable in a partially dehydrated state. As the organs slowly shut down, they cannot process what we healthy people consider a normal amount of food and drink.

I know firsthand this is a really hard concept to grasp. After all, we are conditioned to provide nourishment for the sick. The same concepts do not apply to the *dying* sick.

CHAPTER FOUR

Lover's History

October 7, 2003

I look over at my sleeping husband and realize I could never imagine what my father is going through. He and mom have been happily married for almost thirty-two years. They grew up in neighboring towns in the beautiful rolling hills of southwestern Pennsylvania, and have known each other for more than forty years.

My father, Merle "Max" Cable, is a sweet and simple guy. He is the youngest of four and was raised in a Mennonite home. His deep religious roots, positive attitude, and wonderful sense of humor have served him well over the years. He talks to everyone, no I mean *everyone*...at the grocery store, at the gas station, in elevators. My mom was pretty sociable, too. Must be those small town roots. When I was a child it used to embarrass me when they talked to strangers. Now, I am the same way.

My dad faced the dying process as a child at the age of nine or ten when his mother became terminally ill. He would sit in bed with his mother and play or draw while she wrote in a notebook. I had no idea my grandmother enjoyed writing until I shared the idea of this book with my father. It is interesting to have that connection with a grandmother who died twenty-one years before I was born.

Because he lost his mother at such a tender age, my father was raised by the entire family, including his mother's identical twin sister. What he missed out from his mother, the rest of the family made up for. He will be the first to tell you that he was spoiled. There is not a bitter bone in his body. He does not carry any grudges. His soul is clean and pure. His motto is, "Why worry when you can pray."

Not ready to settle down at the age of twenty-one, my father actually broke my mother's heart when she was a teenager. Raised in the small town of Holsopple, Pennsylvania, my mother was the middle child, the only girl sandwiched between two brothers. In spite of getting less than perfect marks for penmanship (not her fault…she was left-handed) and conduct (she liked to talk…so what?) she made good grades in school. Like many daughters, she had issues with her mother; although she loved her, her dad was her favorite parent. My mother had fallen in love with Merle Cable and so desired to marry him. When she learned he was not ready for marriage, she was devastated. After her high school graduation, she felt her only option other than marriage was nurse's training. She went; she fainted at the sight of the first needle. Okay, that was not going to work.

She had to get away. She did not have many options and moved to one of the Carolinas with an uncle and aunt, and started fresh, away from that small town which had given way to her broken heart. It did not take long for this small town girl to fall for a man in uniform. They were married a few short months later and moved to Connecticut. She was soon pregnant at the age of nineteen. It was during that pregnancy that she received the devastating news of her father's sudden death, and her heart broke again. He died of natural causes...a bad heart. He would never know his daughter's baby, or any of his grandchildren.

My mother ran into Merle at her father's wake, but I never heard much of that story. I suppose it was too long ago, and too painful a time for my mom to remember and share with me.

After giving birth to three baby girls and enduring seven years with a physically abusive husband, my mother was able to get away. She moved back to small town Pennsylvania, and although she was very poor, she had her kids and she had peace. She was surprised when she received a letter from Merle Cable. Word travels fast in a small town. He heard she was back and wanted to visit her. She wrote back, explaining that she was a different person now, and she had three little girls to care for, and she needed time to heal. He wrote back and told her to heal fast; he was coming to visit.

If you know my dad, you know he likes to get his way. I do not mean this to sound negative; it is the typical youngest child syndrome. (My sisters have accused me of being the same way.) He corresponded with her back and forth. Eventually she agreed to see him, and they picked up on their love affair where they had left off about eight years ago. They married less than a year later in January of 1971. My mother later told me how he came to visit her on Thanksgiving Day. As bad timing would have it, she came down with the flu. She had started dinner, but apologized to her male companion and excused herself to just lie down for a few minutes. Apparently he not only finished putting dinner on, he played with her kids and kept them occupied so their mommy could rest. And that is pretty much how my dad lives his life. He is a giver, a doer. He shows his love by doing nice things for people.

My mother took a giant leap of faith by marrying my dad, not only because her first experience with marriage was so rotten, but also because it meant another move away from her family. His job took them to the suburbs of Chicago. Not long after my parents married, I was conceived by pure accident and to my mother's dismay (she wanted to go to work). A few years later my father adopted my mother's three daughters. By that point it was strictly a formality; he had been raising these daughters as his own.

God blessed me with bright red curls and an uncontrollable urge to suck my thumb. Imagine the day we all went to the courthouse so my dad could adopt my sisters. Onlookers must have thought, *"Ah, how nice...this family is adopting a little redheaded orphan who sucks her thumb and hides behind her new mama's leg..."*

As far as I am concerned we pretty much lived happily ever after...dad, mom, Kathy, Patty, Suzie, and me. We were as happy as possible in a home that reared four hormonally imbalanced teenaged girls. I had issues with being so different than my sisters and was extremely shy. Not to mention how mean kids can be when your hair glows in the sun and you have a name that rhymes with a variety of teasing ammunition like "hairy" and "scary." I eventually learned to love being different, but not until I was an adult.

Although we were raised in a Chicago suburb, we connected with our small town roots through annual summer vacations to the beautiful backwoods of Pennsylvania. We spent two weeks each summer on a whirlwind of visits with the different generations of the people who comprised our extended family. It was great fun.

• ❦ •

Somehow I feel lucky in spite of what we are going through as a family. I was raised with lots of laughter and love from two wonderful, solid people. It is a blessing for sure. I am this woman, ME, because of my family, and especially because of her, my sweet mother.

She wants our lives to go on uninterrupted.

That is so ridiculous!

My mother is dying before our eyes...that is NOT normal! My schedule is not normal. My emotions are all over the place. This process is all consuming. I think about it when I wake up in the morning and before I fall asleep at night. Whenever I see a lady out shopping with her mother I am overcome with jealousy. I possess an unending desire to do things with my mother like we used to...to have fun together. Ah, but those days are over; my mother is a very sick woman. The truth hurts.

I am growing. Whatever I am learning I will put in my satchel and carry with me down this road of life.

Somewhere along my journey I will need it. I do not know when or where, nor do I care. I am learning! Thank you, God.

I am looking forward to rediscovering my relationship with my father when...well, when this is "over." There was a time when he did not automatically pass the phone to mom when I called. There was a time before cancer, when I would call just for him. The other night after mom went to bed and the other company left, my husband and I watched TV with dad for half an hour. It was some comedy show involving animals - silly and light – just what we needed.

And I laughed with my father, and for a few minutes we *forgot* about cancer.

And it hit me, really hit home, that I miss my time with my dad, this fun-loving, wonderful man who enjoys life more than anyone I know. The focus has been on mom as necessary of course. This is neither bad nor good, just reality.

Right now I have to spend as much time with my mom as possible. The dying process has taken over my life. I am absorbed in it. I read all the materials hospice provided.

The urge to share my unconditional love with my mother is overwhelming. I do not always know what to say.

"Mom...?"

"Yes?"

We look at each other, and she lets out a sigh. My emotions are burning inside of me, but I cannot express them. I love her, and I feel bad for her, and I want her to know I do not mind helping her. No matter how much I do for her, it is impossible to ever give back all that she has given me over the years. I am devastated that she is dying. She is right here in front of me; and yet I miss her terribly because we cannot go shopping or play games or put puzzles together or even hold a decent conversation anymore.

As I helped her into bed today for the third or fourth or fifth time, she blurted out, "I don't want to live like this...I DON'T WANT TO LIVE LIKE THIS!"

Of course she doesn't! She is growing weaker by the day. These words emerge from a woman who has so bravely, and for the most part cheerfully, battled her illness for years.

"You're entitled to your emotions, Mom, no matter what they are."

Hmm, this is the advice she has offered me so many times when I have struggled...

"Mom, maybe you could think of this time as just a few months, a short time compared to your sixty years."

"Oh, Mare, I hope it's not months. I hope it's days."

I let that sink in. My mom wants to die. She has lost her will to live, to fight. She is tired. The end is near. As I was driving home I thought to myself, *what if my mom died tonight, and I never got to see her again?* I cannot imagine it. Does that mean I am selfish? After all, she is miserable, and we cannot enjoy all the things we used to...and yet I do not want her to die. I do not know quite how to feel about this. Are you ever ready for a dying person to die? I do not know. I have never been here before.

CHAPTER FIVE

Hold the Phone

She sleeps a lot and is too weak to talk on the phone for more than a few minutes, if at all.

This is a great loss for me (and for many who enjoyed mom's gift of gab) as we used to talk on the phone once or twice every day.

Months ago I called her one evening upon discovering a TV show that I thought she might like. We stayed on the phone for over an hour, watching the show together. What fun! What companionship. Lucky me.

I also remember the numerous times the phone rang just as I was walking in the door after a long day at work. My thoughts were focused on bringing in the mail, changing my clothes, and finding something to eat.

"Hello?" I would say in a slightly irritated tone.

My mother's cheerful voice rang out from the other end.

"Hi, Mary!"

She knows I just walked in the door...what does she do, watch the clock?

"Jeez, Ma, I just walked in the door! I've had a long day...can I call you after dinner?"

As I look back, I used to feel guilty for those times – times I was too busy, too wrapped up in myself, or too tired to call her back. The older I get the more I realize guilt is a waste of time. It is normal to feel some guilt, but do not let it take over. Do not spend your days feeling guilty. Spend your days treating others with kindness. My mother used to tell me that every day you should try to do the best that you can. On days when you are a little off, your best will not be as good as the day before, but it will still be the best for that very day. Accept it, and forgive yourself for being human. Learn from your mistakes, forgive those around you, and move on. Enjoy yourself and your life right now. Do not put it off.

She is worried about Al?

Today my mom, in her end-stage state, asked me if Al is doing okay with "this." "This" being me spending so much time with her, away from home, away from work, away from my new husband.

Al Keilman has become one of the best friends I will ever know. He is one of those all around nice guys. He is kind, gentle, strong, sincere, funny, lovable, hard-working, generous, and confident yet humble. He is a terrific looking guy with blue eyes which sparkle in the sunlight. He believes in God and heaven. He loves babies and small children, and they love him, too. He is the kind of guy who smiles a lot. He really listens to people. He cares. He is sympathetic. He is willing to lend a helping hand. He is dependable and a man of his word. I believe everything he does, he does for the betterment of "us." We are a team, partners. I could never express how blessed I am to have him in my life. And to top it off he is a bona fide social butterfly, just like me.

"I just want him to be okay," she said.

About ten months ago my mother spent four weeks in the hospital while they struggled to find the source of her most recent pain. She had unbearable pain in her lower back and hip. Eventually they discovered and radiated a tumor which was pressing on her spine. Without the radiation she could have become incontinent and unable to walk.

Al and I visited her at the hospital on New Year's Eve. I could not hear their conversation, but just before we left he leaned over and gently touched her face as they talked. I let them be. This was between Al and his future mother-in-law. I brought them together; I was the common denominator. But now I respected their one on one conversation belonged just to them. With time my mother came to really trust Al and love him unconditionally. Thank God for that; my mother had high standards for approving my mate.

So when my mother asked me if Al is okay with all of "this," I reassured her he is full of love and patience, and of course he is okay.

How in the world can someone so *dying* be concerned about my husband? Perhaps she thinks if he is okay, he can take care of me, and I will be okay. But I do not know because I cannot ask her. She is too tired for conversation now. The sentences come more slowly and there are less and less of them.

My mother is wonderful!

I do not know how to tell her!

A few months ago when she was able to get around better and lead a somewhat normal life, she came over to our house a few times to spend a couple of days and nights.

Reducing my workload to part time was a difficult decision for me, and I contemplated doing so for months. With the support of my then husband-to-be I began working four days a week instead of five. This allowed me to spend some wonderful quality time with my mom. It was the best decision I ever made. As the months pass I work less and less.

Utilize the Family and Medical Leave Act (FMLA) if you have to. That is what it is for!

Some of the best advice I have to offer is do not hesitate to follow your gut instinct. If you want to spend more time with a loved one, knowing your time is limited, then just do it. Do not let anyone or anything stand in your way. You will have the rest of your life to work, and only a short time to spend with that person.

I am so very thankful I was able to do this. During the days when mom stayed at our house, a couple of times I lay down with her in the middle of the day. It provided an opportunity for some of our last conversations. I would not trade these times for anything; for they are priceless.

On the other hand, if you are not able to be with your loved one because of your job, your family, or because of your own emotional junkyard, it is OKAY! Forgive yourself and get over it. Concentrate on what you CAN do, and do it now.

CHAPTER SIX

She Cannot Join Us Anymore

Early October 2003

My husband and I traveled almost six hundred miles to attend my cousin's wedding last weekend. Two of my sisters, Patty and Suzie, and their families also made the trip. Krysta's wedding was wonderful; it was everything you would expect from a wedding. We all booked rooms at a romantic lodge-type place, deep in the woods of Pennsylvania, which gave way to the reception.

My emotions were overflowing. A wedding is a joyous time, and we were all so grateful to share in this occasion. The bridal party dance was about to start. Everyone looked smashing...to the nines. The lights dimmed, the music started, and all eyes were on the dance floor. Suzie sat across the round table from me with her chair slightly turned out towards the dance floor. I caught a glimpse of her profile and noticed she was blowing her nose...I studied her body language...*is she crying?* She sensed my stare and glanced back at me. I felt the grief in her eye contact. I knew why she was crying. I cried, too. I had to walk away. We missed our mama.

I had just gotten married three months prior; it was nothing short of wonderful. Now my youngest cousin had walked down the aisle. Since she was the last one of the bunch, this great event symbolized a turning point for our generation of cousins. When did we all grow up anyway?

My mother's absence also symbolized a turning point. There *we* were at a major family function, but our *mom* was absent. She was too sick to travel...too sick to enjoy any of this...too dying. For sure, her absence left a void for us daughters.

In spite of the painful void, we were delighted to be there. I reached into my big emotional junkyard and borrowed some happy and some joy and told the man at the counter that I would be back to retrieve my pain when the wedding was over. *This is Krysta and Jeremy's wedding; this day is about them. I will not allow cancer to take that away from us.*

It was so much fun to celebrate with our extended family and appreciate our roots, our foundation. "Good stock," as Uncle Jack would always say and then produce a loud, appreciative, Uncle Jack sort of laugh.

For the remainder of the event, we embraced the occasion. We laughed, and we danced, and we drank a few cocktails. This was a day for family. Our mother would want us to have fun. As Suzie would say, *be in the moment!*

• ☙ •

Our trip home was a safe one. Although the car ride gave way to some much needed down time, I was anxious to get back and see my mom.

How ironic I have found a greater appreciation for her because of cancer...because I realize our days are numbered. C'mon, we all know life is short. But until you KNOW someone is dying...you do not really *know.*

I want my mom. It is such a raw instinct, is it not? I cannot imagine that instinct ever leaves us. I want her when I am sad or happy. She is the first person who comes to mind when something great happens in my life, and I think, *I have got to call my ma...wait until she hears this!*

I cried yesterday at the harsh realization that I will never play Scrabble with her again. I know I should be *thankful* because we played hundreds of times, and I am thankful. But deep down, the little girl inside of me is saying, *I want my mom I want my mom I want my mom right now.* It is so painful to slowly let her go. My heart is breaking.

Today as I held her hand in bed, I carefully chose my words.

"Mom, you have given so much. You have always been there and given your good advice and your love. And because you have given so much, now I have it to give back to you."

"Thank you, Mary."

She grows more frustrated with her failing body. She is very weak and cannot do *anything* by herself anymore. Today somewhere in her slurred speech she used the word humility. But of course. She was always the matriarch of the family, the decision-maker. And now she must depend on us for everything, right down to wiping her, well you know. I can tell you right now, I do not want anyone wiping *my* you-know-what. And yet I do not mind doing it for my very sick mother.

She is in a transition now between being able to get up and being bedridden. She can barely manage a few steps with the walker. We use the wheelchair to take her down the hallway now. She spends a lot of time in her bedroom. When she wants to get up we assist her onto the pot or into the wheelchair. We wheel her down the short hallway to the living room and help her into the recliner chair or hospice bed.

Suddenly a memory floods my mind.

Mom and I are shopping at Hobby Lobby. She is able to walk but uses her wheelchair because her energy is limited. We are goofing off and having fun. I say something funny; she laughs and turns around and looks at me with those twinkling blue eyes which convey a spirit that is very much alive.

I look down at the top of her head now. She sits in the wheelchair, slightly hunched to one side and motionless. She is a lump. Her skin is grayish. *Is this my mother?*

As the end draws nearer, I find it difficult to reach out to others. I know they mean well when they ask how we are doing.

When I am honest with my friends..."Oh, well, mom's not doing so well...you know...it's hard," their facial expressions reveal uneasiness. Perhaps they are remembering their own loved one who died a miserable slow painful awful godforsaken death. It can be awkward.

What am I supposed to say?

"Look, you supportive person, I realize you are trying to be nice to me and show your love and support; however, I don't want to talk about it!"

In my fantasies they reply, *"Mary, your mom is dying and that's a real bummer. Although I am sorry for your unfortunate situation, I do not know what to say, so let's grab a beer or two and not talk about it any more. In fact, if you want, we can pretend the whole thing isn't happening."*

Please do not misunderstand. I certainly do not want to imply that I am unappreciative for their concern. Believe me; I am thankful for all of the support; I just do not want any advice right now. I realize sometimes I need to get things off my chest. That is why I write. I am in a cold dark place where I am most comfortable alone. When I cannot deal with the pain I retreat to a corner of the junkyard, and I cry where no one can see me. I do not want to be comforted. I want to be allowed to feel bad because my mom is dying. She is leaving me. Slowly. Never before have I been this sad.

Sometimes to avoid the topic, when someone asks about her condition, I cheerfully say, "She's fine! Good! Thanks for asking!" And then I change the subject. This is a win-win situation; now neither party has to discuss it.

I go to work less and to care for mom more. She thinks I am wasting my days because she sleeps so much. In spite of her sleep we are running a necessary 24/7 operation of caregiving. I explained it is my choice to be there, so it is not a waste. God knows I would not miss out on this life-changing experience, no matter how painful. When I am not caring for her or cooking or cleaning, I write in my journal. Or I read. My best friend Annie got me hooked on the *Left Behind* series of books. In turn I got my sister Patty hooked on them as well. At least since we are reading the same books we have something other than my mother's ugly disease to talk about.

It is past my bedtime. I must rest so I can take care of my mom. Al is always on me about sleeping and eating regularly. There will be plenty of time for that later. Right now I am dealing with my depression, or whatever it is that I am going through. I did not choose this journey; it chose me. I will walk this path until I come to the end of it. There is no turning back.

I am so glad we moved our wedding up. At the time I dreaded the process; to say the least, rescheduling an entire wedding proved a tedious task. But the rewards were many...my mother was there...and she danced.

These few months of my life seem like an eternity. I cannot imagine a time before this or after this. I have become somewhat reliant on my journal writing as a means to keep my...well, I do not know...maybe as a means for self therapy or something.

So – if you are having a really hard day, try writing your thoughts down as a way to sort them out and purge your soul. If you want you can write about all of the junk you are carrying and then rip the paper into little shreds. Or go outside and scream at the top of your lungs. When your neighbors come out to see what all the commotion is about, look around and say, "Huh, did you guys hear that?" We are human. We need outlets. God gave us all of these emotions, but no manual on how to deal with them.

Journaling has been very therapeutic for me. In fact, most of this book was written totally by accident.

CHAPTER SEVEN

Burn Out

October 24, 2003

Yesterday I received an email from one of my best friends, Penny, who moved to Arizona as an adult. My mother started babysitting for her when we were babies, and we have been attached ever since. Penny expressed her concerns about me getting burned out, and the need to take care of myself.

Although I received Penny's email when I needed it most, I did not completely listen. Her concerns came just a day after another friend was trying to tell me the same thing. Funny, if we would just *listen* to life's clues, our angels would have an easier time doing their job. Patty had also expressed her big-sister opinions about me taking care of myself.

Seems everyone else sensed I was on the verge of burn out. Did I realize I was overtired most of the time? Sure I did. Did I realize I was emotionally unstable? Probably, but I reasoned with myself. My mind processed my exhaustion and desperation, but my heart pressed on.

I have a job to do. I have to help take care of my mother. This is not about me and my selfish needs. This is what you have to go through during the dying process. After my mom dies my life will get back to normal...I think...won't it? I'll be okay. I just have to cry it out. I want to cry all the time now, but my family needs me. They need my support. I wish hospice could give us an idea of how long this will last. How long does my sweet mother have to suffer? I am so tired of being tired.

Once a long time ago my mom told me that when a person gets cancer, the whole family gets it. Now I understand. We suffer as we watch her suffer.

Yesterday I offered to spend the night over at my parents' so my dad could get a good night's rest. It had been a REALLY bad day. My mom forgot she is sick and attempted to walk away - no walker. She became angry with me when I wrapped my arms around her to help her regain her balance. *Well, excuse me, ma.* She often gets frustrated now because of her own confusion with the situation. Anyway, yesterday was just a bad day dealing with things like that.

By the time I got her tucked into bed, I started feeling really antsy. Seriously, my skin was crawling.

I gotta get outta here...I gotta get out of this house. I sat on the single bed in the room next to my mom's. We use baby monitors to alert us when she tries to get up or calls for help. Believe me, when you sleep with the monitor, you sleep with one eye open. Restful it is not.

This bedroom, which served me quite nicely during my very happy childhood, now felt foreign in a way. I looked around the room and remembered the mother who raised me. I slept comfortably knowing she and dad were just a bedroom away. She comforted me after nightmares; she held my head and put a cold rag against the back of my neck during bloody noses. She brought me water if I was thirsty. She offered a calm voice when I was upset or afraid or could not sleep. She even loved me during my teenage years, an amazing feat for sure.

She...*oh dear God, she is gone.* I closed my eyes and wished it all would go away. I could not escape the dark corners of the junkyard. I became aware of my own breathing as my heart rate started to increase. *I gotta go.* I stood. I sat back down. I stood again, facing an inner struggle between knowing I should stay, and realizing I had to get out.

I walked quietly down the hallway and stopped short of the living room. I peeked in to see my father snuggled in the hospice bed. Yes, the hospice bed is meant for mom, but she prefers her own bed for as long as we are able to get her in and out of it. Dad was watching TV, winding down and getting ready for a much needed night's rest.

It was only 7:30 p.m., but we are all overtired and take sleep when we can. We have no schedule. I took another quiet step into the room. He did not notice me. I opened my mouth and tried to find my voice.

"Dad?" I mouthed but only a small noise came out of me. I swallowed and moved closer. My inner battle continued. *I should stay but I just can't.*

"Dad."

He turned to look at me. Suddenly I felt like I was eight again. I was a little girl, and I was going to bring my troubles to my daddy so he could fix them. My sweet father reacted exactly as I knew he would.

"What's the matter, Mary?"

I shook my head and fought the tears. Damn junkyard.

I'm so tired, I thought to myself. I'm so tired of all of this.

"C'mere, honey. What's wrong?"

I was drawn to his side now. I went to him, and he put his hand out to his little girl. I took it.

"Dad, I want to go home. I'm sorry."

"It's okay, Mary," he said as he put his other strong hand over mine.

I shook my head and looked down, wallowing in my self disappointment.

"Listen to me," he said. "You have to take care of yourself. Go home and sleep. Tomorrow is a new day."

"I'm sorry, Dad," I said through my tears.

"Stop, Mary, please. Take care of yourself tonight, honey," he said and then kissed the top of my hand.

I called Patty on the way home and just lost it. She also told me it was okay; I have to take care of myself.

THERE WILL BE PLENTY OF TIME TO TAKE CARE OF MYSELF AFTER MY MOTHER DIES! HOW SELFISH OF ME! NOTHING IS NORMAL RIGHT NOW. It is a horrible thing to go through and I sometimes hate it. I am so tired. I purposely got up early so I can head back over there this morning.

I just want it all to be over. For certain that is not an original thought for someone going through this. My heart aches for my dad. He always looks tired. When mom dies I am going to find his friendship again, and do things with him, like go to the movies or go bowling. What a concept! Do something outside of CANCER!

I have no idea how my dad does it. He is such a good soul. More and more I realize how much I have missed out on doing things with just him because the focus has been on mom. God bless him!

It is hard to find God in all of this, but I know he is there. I believe in heaven, and I believe this is a learning experience. I hope this life lessen proves useful some day because I *hurt*. I cannot express the hurt which now occupies a space in the pit of my core. The hurt for her, to watch her suffer... to watch her dying. The hurt for my family. The hurt I feel when they hurt. The hurt for everyone in the whole wide world who ever watched a love one suffer and die away. We all share the hurt! And somehow time keeps going on while we are suspended in this.

It is nearly 5:30 a.m. I am about to go over; maybe just for the morning and then I will do something different this afternoon. Yeah, right. Maybe Al and I will go out for dinner tonight. Or maybe I will go to the club and get good and drunk. The problem with getting drunk is becoming sober again and realizing now you have a headache to accompany your original sorrows. I have bed head; it is going to be a baseball hat day. Insignificant. Like many things now, simply insignificant.

• ❦ •

Oftentimes my mom is disoriented about the time of day. She wakes up in the afternoon and thinks it is a different day altogether. Or it is 4:00 p.m. and she is convinced it must be midnight. The hospice people tell us this is normal. Well, normal for a *dying* person maybe, but not for me.

The most challenging part about this for us as caregivers is that there is no regular sleep pattern. When she gets up in the wee hours of the morning, the night watchman has to get up, too, because she is a danger to herself.

When I stay, I have to help her out of bed, into the wheelchair, down the hall, and into her recliner. After a little while her eyes grow heavy, and then it is time to do the reverse to help her back into bed. A couple hours later I am stirred from my half-sleep by a rustling noise on the baby monitor. I jump up and scurry to her side, silently telling my little bladder to please hold. I help her out of bed, assist her on the pot, and transfer her into the wheelchair while pushing aside the cobwebs of exhaustion which have formed in my brain. I ignore my weary muscles as I transfer her from the wheelchair to the recliner. I crave sleep or at least conversation if she is going to keep me up at this ungodly hour.

Finally, she speaks. "What time is it?"

"About 3:30 a.m."

"Really?"

"Yes," I say and try to hide a yawn. "Mom, I have to go to the bathroom. I'll be right back…I promise."

When I return she asks, "What time is it again?"

"The middle of the night."

"Huh, I could swear it was the middle of the afternoon."

"I know, Mom."

"Well," she says as she raises her eyebrows, "you got any pie?"

In spite of my weariness, I gladly serve up the pie. I try to remind myself that my weariness is temporary, but her illness is not. I feed the pie to her in small bites. She cannot seem to get the fork and the food into her mouth at the same time, so we help her. A dish towel serves nicely as a bib across her chest.

Dad is the one who suffers with night duty exhaustion the most. During the early weeks he would leave soon after someone arrived in the morning. He needed to fly the coop, walk around the hardware store or visit his friend Bill. But now he is too tired. When we arrive in the morning he goes straight to bed, but we know he will not completely catch up on his sleep until this is over.

It is painful to witness both of my parents struggle through this.

My mother is (was?) an avid stamp collector. The other day she asked me to put her collection of buffalo stamps and stuff together into a book, so I have been working on that project here and there. It is a small project compared to the "birds around the world," which I completed mostly on my own because my mother wanted it done and could not do it herself. She really tried to get me interested in stamp collecting over the years. I took her to a few stamp shows, but it never truly peaked my interest.

My mom's eyesight is failing. I hand her a stamp and a magnifying glass, and say something cheerful, like, "Wow, look at the beautiful colors in this one, Ma!" After moving the magnifier back and forth, she hands it back to me, shakes her head, closes her eyes, and dejectedly says, "that's enough…I just can't see it." She knows she can no longer enjoy her hobbies. She does not want to live like this. I feel so sorry for her.

I do not want to let her go, yet I do not want her to suffer. I wish I could share her pain, her illness. I would take it from her.

She can only watch TV for a few minutes at a time, and she does not like to listen to music anymore. It makes her nervous and keeps her awake. She cannot stand to be in the middle of more than a couple of people having a conversation. What a change! She was always the story teller in the family and loved to capture everyone's attention. Hmm, guess I got it honest.

CHAPTER EIGHT

Reach Out For Help

Lois, the hospice social worker, has been a great help to me and my family. I would recommend to anyone who is going through something like this (or going through anything tough in your life) to reach out to the help that is offered. Let's face it. They are professionals. They are seasoned. They have dealt with the dying process and how it affects the whole family. Let them help you. Do not carry this weight by yourself.

Years ago, my mother went to counseling as an adult to work through some issues she needed help with. I believe in my heart, because she made the decision to resolve these issues within herself, she lived a more peaceful life, and therefore was a better all around person.

When I first met Lois, I immediately put up a brick wall. She was a stranger. In my opinion, she had no idea what we were going through. Boy, was I wrong.

She knew exactly what we were going through... where we had been and where we were headed. One day I let down my guard and decided to give Lois a chance. I had nothing to lose. I would allow myself to open up to her, and if I did not like her advice, it would be the first and the last time I would talk about all of this. She won me over. She listened. She was insightful. She could see that I was trapped in the junkyard, and helped me temporarily escape. In fact, she helped me develop a healthier way of thinking for the rest of my life. So reach out. You have nothing to lose. To all of the social workers out there, God bless you.

Lois also helped me with the junk I was carrying about my sister Kathy moving. The week after I got married, she happily announced that they had found a home and were moving to another state.

What?

We were all pretty surprised by the news. My parents considered themselves lucky that all four of their daughters had settled within an hour of each other. We spent birthdays and holidays together. When I was younger and single I spent many summer evenings at Kathy's house, playing with my nieces and nephews, passing the time playing games or working a puzzle. Kathy's door was always open. She was a staple in my life. She was there when I needed her. And now, just like that, she and her husband decided to move to another state. I did not get it. I had mixed emotions about the move, not only for my selfish reasons of wanting to keep the family together, but also because my mom was so sick. I was apprehensive that Kathy would need her mom, just like we all did, and she would be too far away to just drop by and see her and soak up whatever she had left in her to give her daughters.

I poured it all out to Lois one day. She helped me realize that it was okay that Kathy moved. Kathy was excited about her new place, and there were reasons why they moved when they did. Fortunately they were only a couple of hours away, so they could visit when they felt the need.

Lois helped me see the dying process from an outside perspective. As humans, we see things all the time from our *own* perspective. My reality comes from my perspective. What I think is normal is what my self tells me is normal. My normal is different from my sister's normal. Lois helped me see Kathy's perspective, and I had a better understanding of why she moved.

People deal with the dying process in different ways. *My* way of dealing with it is being right there in the middle of it, every day, learning about the different medications, learning about the dying body and what to expect, soaking up every last bit of conversation mom has left, helping her in and out of bed, cooking for her, doing laundry, etc. This would be *no* different if Kathy had not moved away. Maybe she would be around to help us with the cooking, but so what? Shoulda, coulda, woulda.

If anything I feel more sympathetic towards Kathy because she is far away. That has got to be tough. Being able to care for my mother is a *gift*. If I am there a lot and I am tired, that is *my choice*. I should not resent others for not being there as much. I felt a lot lighter when I let the resentment go. I will be much more content in this life if I do my own thing and let others do theirs. Who am I to judge? Seriously.

My sister Kathy has a big heart. Over the years, when I was too busy to spend more time with my mom because I was too wrapped up in myself, or my job, or my friends, or whatever boyfriend I had at the time, Kathy was always there for her. Whatever time they were meant to spend together, they did. Moving away does not take that away. Kathy has a great relationship with our mom. I am so thankful that I opened up to Lois, and she helped me celebrate my mom and Kathy's love for one another. Doesn't that sound a lot healthier than carrying resentment? I love my sister Kathy. I love all of my sisters. We are so different, and yet so alike. No distance can break our common threads.

If you find yourself carrying resentment, let it go. It is not healthy and will accomplish nothing. Try to realize that whatever you are going through now, although painful, is meant to be...it is part of your life path.

CHAPTER NINE

Some Final Words of Wisdom

November 17, 2003

"My mother came down from heaven, and I would like to have a conversation with her."

"What'd you say, Mom?"

"My mother."

"What about her?"

"I'm telling you…my mother was here, and I want to ask the nurse about maybe taking less morphine so I can stay awake and feel a little smarter and visit with her."

"Was it a hallucination?"

"No, I really don't think so."

There is no way to know if my dead grandma truly visited from heaven. A few times we heard noises on the baby monitor, and upon going into mom's room found her sound asleep. Explain that? One of my cousins insisted grandma was in her hotel room the night before I got married, assuring her I was doing the right thing. I have heard several stories to support that our loved ones who have passed help us with the transition from the physical existence to the spiritual one. I suppose I will just have to wait and see for myself some day.

Patty, mom, and I all agreed and expressed out loud that today was a good day in spite of the fact that my mother cried a lot.

"Mom, what's the matter?"

Through her tears she woefully said, "Something happened this morning. I realized your dad slept with me all night. He held my hand. Before last night I did not want him to be close to me because then we will be apart, and I can't bear it!" As she sobbed Patty and I started to cry.

Later as I helped her into bed I said, "Mom, it is normal for a dying person to want to withdraw from their loved ones."

"How do you know this?!" she asked, surprised.

"I read all about the dying process in a pamphlet that hospice gave us."

She started crying again and in an almost childlike manner demanded, "You never read it to me and I want you to read it to me!"

So I did. She told dad to sit with us; he perched on the bedside commode. I sat next to her in bed, and out of the corner of my eye I watched my tender-hearted father silently cry as I read aloud the things to expect of a dying person.

Later with Patty present mom made me read it aloud again, which seemed redundant to me but I did it anyway. When I was done she told Patty she had seen a small child bobbing around behind her, only to realize it was her little black dog, Silkie, and then she laughed genuinely. Like I said, she realizes she hallucinates.

She told us each, individually, that she had something to say.

To dad, to me, to Patty.

Her voice was serious with sincerity. "I'm sorry if I was ever mean to you while you were taking care of me. I realized this morning that I need your forgiveness, and such forgiveness will be a big event."

"Mom, it's *okay*. I do forgive you if you were ever in a bad mood, but forgiving you is easy, Mom. Really," I said.

"Really?"

"Yes, Mom," Patty said.

"Oh," she cried out, "I thought you would have to decide whether you would forgive me or not, and it would be a big deal!"

Not so.

I would be lying if I said my mother never hurt my feelings through all of this. There were many days when I was trying so hard to please her, to care for her, and she took out her frustrations on me. She has said hurtful things to me, my father, my sisters.

But the love she has given us all these years far outweighs any end-stage crabbiness.

I lay in bed with her today. We were both on our left sides; she had her back to me. So many times growing up I would lie down in this very spot with my back to her as she ran her fingers through my hair or made spider fingers up and down my back. *"Mommy, do the spider! Do the spider!"*

I looked at her. She is my mama, my mommy. She is so familiar, the way she looks, the way she is positioned, the way she smells. I looked at her thin, silver hair. I wanted to touch her but I did not want to disturb her. I lay very close to her and listened to her slow, labored breathing. I contemplated what to say.

"I love you, Mom."

"I love you, too."

"You're a good mother."

"You're a good daughter."

"It's easy to be a good daughter when you have a good mother."

A slight pause.

"Ah, it's easy to be a good mother when you have a good daughter. Now go away and let me rest."

Later on mom said we could write things for people to say to each other. She was referring to the nice things we had expressed while in bed. Patty has also mentioned we should write a book about this. Maybe we should.

Yes, today is a good day. Patty and I wonder if all of mom's conversation today is the "surge of energy" not long before death.

• ❦ •

Later the same day

Today was unusual in that mom could enjoy the company of a whole group at the same time. Late this afternoon we gathered around her in the living room. It was me, Patty, Betty (our hospice nurse), dad, and Patty's daughter, my sixteen-year-old niece, Karlie. Dad explained how mom asked him to lay in bed with her the night before and just hold her hand. They fell asleep like that.

Karlie, having grown up next door to my parents, shares a special bond with her grandma and grandpa.

Karlie began to cry. Really cry. She buried her face in her mother's side, and Patty held her and comforted her.

I saw a mix of emotions on my mother's face. I am sure she felt bad for being the cause of her granddaughter's tears. I have an idea what was going through my mom's head. As relatives passed away over the years, and I grieved, my mother always told me that when her dad died she realized life is short. We are all going to die, and we must eventually learn the painful lesson of grief, which accompanies death and the dying process.

I will never forget what my mom said to Karlie today. She took a deep breath, cocked her head slightly, and very gently said,

"Karlie."

Karlie turned from her mother and looked at her grandmother. They held eye contact for a long moment.

"Just remember what a good life I've had. This is sad, but it would be a hundred times worse if we were sitting here talking about *you* being sick. Okay?"

Karlie gave her grandmother a tearful nod of understanding as we all sat for a moment, fixated on mom, the matriarch of our family, *digesting what we know will be some of her last words of wisdom.*

CHAPTER TEN

Thankful For Family... Thankful For Memories

As the baby of the family I suppose I had some "youngest child" advantages while growing up. First of all, my parents got to practice on my sisters before they got to me. Secondly I learned from my sisters' mistakes. For instance, one summer a sister who will remain nameless got grounded for kissing a boy in the garage while my parents were away. Therefore I learned if you are going to kiss a boy do not do it in the garage. Thirdly, by the time I became a teenager my parents were simply too tired to wait up for me. Fortunately for them I was a good kid and *usually* made my midnight curfew.

One of the biggest advantages, though, comes as an adult. Long after my mom is gone, I will rely on my big sisters to remind me of her good advice, help me with her recipes, teach me how to put a certain quilt patch together, comfort me when I am sick, and join me in making new memories. Even at a time when I am so sad, I am able to reach down and remind myself of these things.

We sit here, Patty and I. She is reading, and I am writing this. Patty is the second in line of our sisters and eight years older than I am. Years ago after she moved out and got married, she and her husband Patrick (cute, isn't it? "Pat and Patty") would pick me up and let me tag along for a day and spend the night at their house which they affectionately referred to as "the shack." Her husband Pat drove an older white Plymouth Valiant which had typical 1960's ocean blue bench seats, and I got to share the back seat with their red Doberman pinscher, Sheila. When we were sitting down, that dog was bigger than me and apparently not used to sharing the back seat. She would smile and pant and stick her front paws into the side of my little leg. The more I moved over the more she stretched out, until eventually I was crammed upside the car door, with one arm reached up around Sheila's neck. She was so close I could feel her warm doggy breath.

"Is Sheila crowding you back there, Mary," my sister would say more as a statement than as a question while glancing over her shoulder.

The problem with going to Patty's was I was terrified of sleeping by myself in a strange room in a strange house. It never occurred to me that hello, they have a guard dog, and often I lay there, wide-eyed in the dark, listening to every sound the shack had to offer. I guess the boogie man took those nights off, though, because when morning came I found myself safe and still all in one piece.

Although Patty is a few inches shorter than I am, we probably look the most alike. We inherited our mother's apple cheeks and soft bodily edges. That is a nice way of saying that what we put into our mouths is directly correlated to our waist size. A few years ago when Patty was training to walk a marathon, she went to see her doctor because she was exercising a lot and dieting, and yet she could not shave off those few extra pounds. After testing her thyroid and determining it was normal, the doctor told her to blame it on genetics.

"Genetics!" she exclaimed.

"No way!" I replied.

"Yep! If you see mom before I do tell her thanks for the fat genes!"

Pat and Patty eventually upgraded their habitat and bought the house next door to my parents, which is a little ironic since she was always the one to fight with our mother. She can be a real fire ball but has calmed down as of lately. She is white collar during the week and rides her Harley with her husband on the weekends. She loves dogs and has a knack for training them. Over the years whenever she lost one she always seemed to get another. Currently she has three, not to mention the cat. She has a great sense of humor, and we laugh all the time. Over the years she clashed heads mostly with our mom, but that is normal for mothers and daughters. With time they have forgiven each other and realized probably one of the reasons they clash is because they are so much alike. Go figure. Her experience as a nurses' aide brings her front and center in caring for our mom.

Suzie is the third sister, the one right before me. There are four years which separate us, so as kids we were either playing very nicely together or arguing over something which held great meaning to us, such as who got the bigger serving of Kool-Aid. My parents were smart in finding a solution to this. They let one kid pour and the other one choose which cup she wanted. I remember when it was *my* turn to pour I would eye the amounts and then pour two more drops into this one, and then into that one. I was not about to let my big sister tell me I was too little to pour even amounts as she gloated over choosing the bigger serving.

By trade Suzie is a school teacher and currently substitutes in between raising my three perfect nieces, who are too young to completely understand what is going on. She lives about an hour away and manages to come and help once or twice a week.

Somehow she maintains normalcy for her little daughters and their little lives. I do not know how she does it. Maybe she only visits the dark corners of her junkyard in the shower when she is alone, or late at night as her husband holds her after her children have drifted off to their happy dream places.

CHAPTER ELEVEN

Her Friends

November 20, 2003

Maria Mendoza lived kiddy-corner to us and was my babysitter from as far back as I can remember. She and her husband Jesse provided a home away from home for me, a safe haven so to speak. Maria and Jesse's house was (and still is!) full of their own children and now grandchildren. Because Maria was filled with love and patience, she had the makings of a good babysitter. We knew she loved us, and she kept us entertained. We never left the house as a group before holding hands in the kitchen to pray for a safe outing. From an adult perspective it is obvious why my mom felt so at ease leaving me in the hands of our beloved Maria.

Thankfully I was too little to realize how much I stood out when they let me tag along to different places. Maria's children had beautiful olive skin and silky dark hair. My skin would glow bright pink if I stayed in the sun for more than ten minutes. If you added up all of the minutes over the years, I must have spent hours of my childhood sticking my arms and legs out so an adult could slather me with sunscreen.

My mom and Maria became fast friends. They shared a love for quilting and often helped each other with different projects. When my mom had a quilt in the frame it took up a good part of our living room. I remember many times crawling underneath to play with a friend while mom and Maria sat and quilted.

A couple Saturdays ago Maria and Jesse came to visit their dying friend. Later mom told me why it was so important for them to visit on that very day; it was the anniversary of the death of their baby daughter. She died many years ago as a tiny infant. I remember that awful event as a child, but I was too young to understand the true devastation.

Maria and Jesse came to tell mom how much she meant to them, how they will never forget what wonderful support she provided during that trying time. The next day I lay in bed with mom, and we talked about it.

"One time after they lost that baby," she said, "Jesse called and said he did not know what to do with Maria."

"Oh?"

"She was very depressed, and Jesse asked if I would please come over to see her."

I lay there, looking at the ceiling, picturing my Maria as she was in her younger years, in anguish over losing her little baby. We expect old people to die, but not babies.

My mom continued, "I dropped what I was doing and went right over. Jesse greeted me at the door and told me she was in the bedroom. I found her in bed crying. I just crawled right in and comforted her."

"Oh, Mom," I said, "I never knew that!"

"Maria and Jesse are good people. We are lucky to have them."

Her story touched me and caused me to reflect on my own friendships. When mom was there to comfort her friend, she was a little older than I am now. Relating to her as an adult, woman to woman, is a wonderful enlightenment to my soul. Yes, this is where I come from. I realize more and more how thankful I am to have her as a mother, to be so lucky to have been raised with such love and morality.

Maria called today. "How's your mom today, Mary?"

"Okay I guess. She sleeps a lot, Maria. How are you?"

"Oh, I'm fine. Jesse and I are getting ready for our vacation to Missouri. We wanted to come see your mother before we left."

"Well, I don't know, she is probably sleeping."

"I know, honey, but we should really see her before we leave."

I got it. They wanted to see her in case she died while they were away.

"Okay, let me go talk to her and see if I can wake her up."

"Okay, I'll hold on."

I left the phone on the kitchen table and ventured into the living room where my mom rested in the hospice bed.

"Mom."

Nothing.

"Mom." I was just slightly louder than the first time.

Nothing. I stared at her very still body. Her skin was gray. Her eyes were closed. She was perfectly silent. She looked like a dead person. I was not alarmed; she often looked like this. I waited several seconds, and finally her chest and belly moved as she released a very noisy breath. *Nope, she's not dead.*

I placed a gentle hand on her soft arm and got just a little bit louder. After all, I did not want to scare her to death. (Pun intended.)

"MOM."

"Hmm?" she said as she turned her head in my direction and raised her eyebrows but did not open her eyes.

"Maria is on the phone. They want to see you."

She did not say anything at first, and I thought maybe she would be unable to find her sentences today. After a long moment she said, "You know something, Mary? When people are dying, it takes a lot of courage to not back away from them." She opened her eyes. "Tell them to come on over."

My heart aches for people like Maria, who is losing a friend...to cancer. Margo Winston is another one of those friends. She is definitely the sister my mother never had. She calls daily.

I always loved going over to the Winston's as a child. Margo's daughter Pam was a year older than me, and we played well together so the grownups could visit. My dad became good friends with Margo's husband, Bill, so it was a good match all around. Margo was also a quilter and big time crafter, so there was always some sort of project in the works.

The Winston household offered two things that I did not have at my house...a crawl space and little brothers. I was intrigued by both. The crawl space under the basement was scary at first, but I soon overcame my fear when I learned it gave way to a variety of games and toys that would provide hours of playtime entertainment. As far as the little brothers, I enjoyed their company even when Pam wanted to chase them away. When she tired of her little brothers, she would say, *"This is a girl's game...go upstairs and play!"* I liked these younger siblings; our house lacked not only little brothers, but little siblings of any sort. At Margo's house I could join Pam in the bossing around of these little beings, and send them away when they refused to follow our rules or became annoying or too rambunctious. The only one at our house that I could boss around was our fat little Dachshund-Terrier mix, Cleo, and whenever I became too bossy with her she would hide from me under the antique cedar chest in the living room.

I am certain my regular popcorn cravings stem from those visits at Margo's. Her popcorn was always better than our popcorn. She popped it in oil, drowned it in butter, and topped it off with a sprinkle of salt. She would fill a big bowl to almost overflowing, and we kids were allowed to take it down to the basement where we did not have to share with the adults. No offense to my mother and her little air popper, but Margo had her beat in the popcorn category.

In spite of her illness, mom worries so much for Margo. Over the years she and her family have experienced some very painful losses of their own. Mom worries about Margo and her bad knees, and about Bill, who has recently suffered with health complications of his own. Yes, my dying mother worries about her best friend. What a sweetheart indeed. And Margo worries about her, too. These women know they will soon be apart.

I suppose in addition to my mother's physical challenges, she, too, is experiencing emotional turmoil. She has to leave Margo and Maria and my dad and all of us. She told me once that she cannot imagine going to a place away from all of us. I never thought of it that way. I always think of all of us learning to live without her; but at least I know I will still have my dad, my sisters, my friends, my familiar life. She is facing the unknown. She will rely on her religion now more than ever.

CHAPTER TWELVE

Keep the Humor

It is truly amazing how my mother's sense of humor still comes through in bits and pieces. The other day she asked me to pluck out the few hairs which grow on her upper lip. Talk about up close and in your personal space.

"I'm sorry if this hurts, ma," I said as I used a tweezers to pluck the little hairs. I had a hard time seeing them as they are very light in color.

"No, it's fine. It's doesn't hurt."

"Okay."

She held very still and looked away; then I felt her looking at me.

"What?" I asked.

"I was just thinking...you could do this for me before they take me away."

"What?" I asked as I backed away a few inches.

"You know what I mean," she said as she raised her eyebrows slightly and grinned.

"Very funny."

"I'm serious!" she said.

"Okay, ma."

"Don't let me down, Mary," she said and winked.

I thought, *I'll make sure you don't have any whiskers showing when you are in your casket with your hair done and your pretty blue dress on. Noted.*

Another time recently Patty helped her sit up in bed because she was choking. She coughed and coughed as Patty gently patted her on the back. She looked at Patty and said, "Great! Now I'm shitting! I'm totally shitting!" Patty, stifling her laughter, looked at her and said, "It's okay, Mom. I put something under you so you wouldn't soil the bed."

Mom sighed a sigh of relief and said, "Oh, you're a wonderful, lovely person," to which Patty replied, "You're a wonderful person too, Mom."

As it turned out, mom was not "totally shitting;" however, she did grace Patty with a little flatulence. Patty and I laughed so hard when she told me about this; it was hilarious!

Do not be afraid to find humor in your experiences, no matter what life presents. I make a point to store a lot of humor in the junkyard no matter what else may be taking up space at the time. Sometimes you have to laugh just to get through the day.

As the end draws nearer, her ability to communicate severely diminishes. So when she speaks, we pay close attention. When she awoke one morning recently I told her Margo was coming for a visit. I did not expect a reply. Surprisingly, she found her voice.

"Good," she exclaimed, "tell her to hurry or she may be too late!"

"She's on her way, Mom."

Mom and Margo have always shared their humor, so why should that change now? I told Margo what my mother had said about telling her to hurry, and we had a good laugh over that too.

While Margo sat at mom's bedside, chatting, Patty leaned over close to mom's face and gently applied Chap Stick to her dry lips. Mom rubbed her lips together, and Patty very sweetly said, "Does that feel good, Mom? Would you like some more?"

Again, to our surprise, she found her voice.

"No! And stop interrupting Margo!"

It was so unexpected we all burst into laughter.

Here is this woman, weak, dying, her body and mind failing, her voice failing most of the time, and yet she was still able to set her ground as the matriarch, the mother-boss of the family, throwing out an order to be quiet.

CHAPTER THIRTEEN

It Is Getting Closer

November 23, 2003

Mom requires more and more assistance walking and transferring in and out of bed, the recliner chair, the wheelchair.

She eats less and less. One of her favorite things to eat is salmon patties and asparagus. That may sound strange, but I cook it for her lunch at least once a week. Because her mouth is so dry, I cut up half of a salmon patty into very small bites. Then I cut up one piece of asparagus into very small bites, drown it all in asparagus juice and mix it up together. She likes it a lot but does not ever eat it all. She does not eat much of anything anymore, so if this is something that she can enjoy I would cook it for her every day if she wanted it. Plus I like to eat salmon patties so I get lunch out of it, too.

Today she enjoyed a visit with my friend, Caitlyn, whom she had not seen since the wedding. We all sat in the living room and chatted for just a few minutes. As usual, exhaustion took over, and mom could not stay awake. With our trusty wheelchair I helped her into the bedroom, tucked her in, and rejoined the group which now gathered around the kitchen table. I sat across from my husband with my back to the hallway. Suddenly his eyes grew wide; he was looking past me. I looked over my shoulder to see my feeble mother leaning against the hallway. She had a smile on her face. I am sure she heard us chatting and came to join the fun. I jumped up as quickly as I could and barely kept her from falling. I helped her into the bathroom and wrapped my arms around her so she would not sit down too hard on the pot.

She forgets to use her bedside commode. She forgets she should not get out of bed by herself. She forgets she can barely walk.

"Mom, you should really not get out of bed by yourself. Especially since last week you fell down... remember? We are all here to help you, Mom. We don't want you to get hurt, so please, call for help. That's why we are here, Mom...okay?"

She did not say anything.

"Okay?"

Without looking at me she replied, "Yeah, but then I wouldn't get this lecture every time."

How can I blame her for resisting giving up her independence? She has been a fighter all her life, sixty years worth. Why would she change now? The problem is she can be a real danger to herself. My father heard her in the bathroom one day last week, and by the time he reached her it was too late. She fell over head first into the bathtub. He fished her out and was thankful all of her bones were intact. She was very lucky. The cancer is everywhere in her bones. A scan indicated twenty-two places, to be exact; that was four years ago.

The confusion worsens. She has asked more than one of us, exactly what does she have, and is she dying, and how long has she been sick? More than once she insisted my father get her out of bed because it was her wedding day. Then she would sit in the recliner with her eyes closed and move her arms around and act as if she went to a different time, a different place. The hospice handbook tells me this behavior is "normal." Supposedly when people are dying they revisit different life events in their mind, and it actually becomes part of their reality.

"Max," she told my dad one time, "Put Silkie up here on my lap." Silkie is one of her prized little dogs. Silkie was glad to be on her mama's lap, and probably wonders why her mama sleeps so much. Mom petted her and petted her. "She's so soft, isn't she?" she said happily.

"Yes, she is, honey."

"I want to ride on her."

"What did you say, honey?"

"Silkie. I want to ride on Silkie."

At that my father held back a giggle. "Oh, Arlene, I think Silkie is too small and too tired for you to ride on her."

"Really?"

"Yes, but she loves it when you pet her." He went to my mother's side then and ran his gentle hand over Silkie's back. He kissed his confused sweetheart on the forehead. She looked up at him, smiled, and stuck her chin out while forming her lips into a kissy face. He kissed her and smiled and petted their little dog. "Nice Silkie. Nice Silkie."

One morning when I arrived she looked at me wide-eyed and said, "Oh, Mary! Thank God you're here! What happened? How long have I been here? How long have I been sick?"

I gently placed my hand on her arm, looked into her blue eyes, and said, "Mom, you have a return of breast cancer. You got breast cancer about twelve years ago. Then you were okay for a long time before it came back in your bones..."

She closed her pretty eyes, turned her head slightly away from me, and lay back in bed.

"Okay, okay," she interrupted, "I remember now. I remember."

She remembered she is dying.

How sad is that.

• ♡ •

And Closer
December 2, 2003

She has not eaten anything since last Thursday, Thanksgiving dinner. I suppose if someone were to choose a last meal, Thanksgiving dinner would be a good choice. Of course this is thanks to Patty. She has cooked Thanksgiving for mom and dad and whoever else wanted to stop by for many years.

This year I did not cook. I did not care. Al and I joined two of our friends for an extravagant buffet at a hotel. I stuffed myself in an attempt to temporarily appease the junkyard dog. It was a surreal escape from reality as we ate, talked, smiled, and enjoyed the live musical talent of a male Asian violinist. We even had our picture taken with him. I appear happy in the picture.

Afterwards Al and I went to my parents' house. For me our holiday visit held no holiday spirit.

The pain traveled up the right side of her face that cold Thursday in late November.

"My right eye hurts."

This was a new challenge.

"Okay, Mom, I'll get you some morphine," Patty said as she went into the kitchen to retrieve the medication. I followed her and said in a slightly hushed voice, "Patty, I just gave her some morphine five minutes ago. Is this safe?"

"Maybe it didn't kick in yet," she replied.

I followed my sister back into the living room.

"Mom, Mary said you just had some morphine five minutes ago. Why don't we give it ten more minutes and see if you feel a little better, okay?"

"Okay," she said. "Turn off that TV! I can't stand it any more!"

Al fumbled with the remote and managed to turn off the football game. This would not go down in history as one of the Cable's traditional Thanksgivings. *The holidays mean nothing to me this year. I hate the holidays. My mother is in a lot of pain right now, and we have to somehow fix her.*

"I might as well go to bed," she said and tried to push down the foot rest of the recliner chair. Patty leaned over right away and helped her click it into place. Al and Suzie's husband, Steve, quietly excused themselves to the kitchen.

She was disgusted not only with the pain but also with her inability to enjoy the daughters, sons-in-law, and grandchildren who had come for a final Thanksgiving visit.

We helped get her from the living room into the bedroom. Patty, Suzie, and I gathered around our little dying mother as she lay in bed.

"It still hurts," she said. We gave her some more morphine. And then some more. And then some more. We called hospice, and they gave us permission to give her as much as she needed to be free of the pain.

Poor mom!

The hours seemed like an eternity. She was definitely getting worse, but we eventually got the pain under control. At one point my mother wanted me to call the doctor and ask for something to relieve a sinus infection. I tried to tell her it probably was not a sinus infection, and that she should take some more morphine. She insisted I make a phone call, not knowing that we already talked to the hospice nurse, who explained the disease is most likely traveling up.

Yuck.

So I *lied* to my mother and told her I would go in the other room to call the doctor. I reappeared after a few minutes and told her the doctor said it is not her sinuses, and that she needed more morphine *right now.*

My mother has been complaining about a tickle on her upper lip. I examined it and washed her face and determined there was nothing there. The nurse explained there is possibly some nerve damage in her face. One day recently one of mom's eyes started to wander. I do not know how else to put this...it is weird, okay. Her eyes go in different directions. It is awful to look into my mother's eyes and not see her.

This cancer is a real b**ch!

Thanksgiving weekend was a challenge to say the least. By Friday we were calling hospice for assistance with a mother who was becoming so weak we could hardly transfer her out of bed, as her weary legs could no longer sustain her.

By Monday they had doubled her pain medication, the long acting morphine (in pill form), and again assured us it was okay to give her as much of the liquid morphine as she needed. We also gave her a certain liquid medicine which I will refer to as the "resting medicine." (I do not want to use actual drug names here as I believe the pharmaceutical companies are powerful enough to do their own advertising.)

When she could not swallow anymore, we learned she would have to ingest the pill a different way, through the *other* end. Yes, this is what you do because your mother requested to die at home. And we *want* her at home. In my opinion, Patty should get the job. She was a former nurses' aide, right? She should be used to sixty-year-old behinds. I will never forget the morning Patty called me and said, "Well, I hope you're happy...I just shoved a pill up mom's ass!"

We had to laugh.

Laugh or cry.

Take your pick.

CHAPTER FOURTEEN

Bedridden

She stays in the living room now. We are unable to safely get her into the wheelchair and therefore unable to get her into her bedroom. We transfer her from the hospital bed to the recliner chair by completely lifting her in a bear hug fashion.

She used to help us by hugging back but now she is unable to do even that. She can hardly move her limbs any more. Her head is a heavy weight. Her skin is getting grayer. She cannot swallow anything anymore.

Today when I gave her the liquid morphine and the resting medicine she choked a little. Some trickled down her throat instead of staying under her tongue, and she attempted to cough but could not. Now she rattles...she is noisy. Yikes. I offered her some water but got no response.

The death rattle. I have heard of this. It is gross. It is eerie, almost inhuman. I imagine the death rattle must have been very loud at night when my sweet father was alone in the house with her, trying to sleep on the couch next to his dying wife.

When you go through something like this with someone you love, with all your heart you want to do the right things for them. You want to grant their every wish. You want to utilize the medication to keep them comfortable, out of pain and well rested without over-medicating them and sending them into a drug-induced existence.

I was concerned about this over the weekend as mom's morphine was *doubled* to sixty milligrams in a twenty-four hour period. We are talking heavy duty narcotics here. Her speech is failing; sometimes she tries to talk and simply groans. When I apologize to her and tell her I do not understand, she gets agitated and tries to get out of bed.

From the hospice material I learned it is common for a person to get agitated easily due to a lack of oxygen in the body when they are within a few days of dying. The other day she told me I was trying to kill her. She also told Patty if she did not get her out of bed she was going to kick her. Patty and I have both explained to her that we physically cannot get her in and out of bed all the time because we are going to hurt ourselves or hurt her.

The last time we got her into the recliner she could hardly sit up. We had to prop her with a pillow on one side, and, although she slept, she looked horribly uncomfortable. Her head was not positioned just right or something. And her arms seemed out of place. It was awful. It makes me want to throw up, really, when I think about it. It was like something out of the movie *Weekend at Bernie's,* but the dead guy in the movie never looked this bad. We decided we should get her back into bed.

As I lifted her with all my might and transferred her back into bed, my mother spoke to me for the last time.

"I'm going to fall!" she groaned in an unfamiliar voice. Yes, those were my mother's last words to me.

With my arms holding her around her mid-section, I sat her as gently as I possibly could on the bed and went down on my knees in front of her. I hugged my mama around her soft middle and quietly said, "Mom, I promise I will not drop you."

I was pained by her grave and confused expression. Her mouth hung open. She tried to focus on me, but there again; there is the issue with the wandering eyes. She looked at me and then looked up and away and blinked a couple of times. She seemed very far away. I lifted her little legs into the bed and moved her body into a lying position. I have no idea whether she was comfortable or not. I tucked her in anyway and kissed my far-away mama on the forehead and told her how much I love her.

I am not sure if she knows who we are anymore, or if she knows where she is, or who she is. She does not look like Arlene Cable when her eyes go like that.

Anyway, because of her inability to speak, to reason, to understand she is too weak to get out of bed, I was concerned of over-medicating her. I was hoping the nurse would tell us we could back off of the morphine, and mom would be more like mom.

I made up a fantasy in my mind of a would-be conversation with our nurse.

Betty and I stand at mom's bedside. Betty is dressed like a 1950's nurse with the funny hat, A-line skirt, white hose and white sneakers.

"Betty, I think we are giving her too much morphine."

"Really? Why?"

"Look at her. She sleeps and groans and her eyes wander in different directions. Isn't there something we can do? I am afraid that maybe we are overmedicating her."

"Oh dear," Betty replies, "Let's take a look at her medication log."

After reviewing the log, Betty cheerfully says, "You're right!" and rushes to my mother's side. "Arlene, can you hear me?" She gently shakes her arm, and my mother opens her eyes, her beautiful sparkling normal blue eyes.

"Arlene, there has been a mistake! No more morphine! Get up! You're okay!"

Suddenly my mother jumps out of the hospice bed, and the three of us hold hands and dance in a circle around the living room.

"I feel good," she says, surprised at the discovery of her regular voice. "I can talk and I can see!"

Back in the real world, I did in fact express my concerns about too much morphine to Betty, our nurse (notice I say "our" nurse – the hospice folks really cater to the entire family...thank God for them). She assured us that the amount of morphine mom takes is not enough to cause such behavior. It is the disease...the natural progression of the disease. THE DYING OF THE PHYSICAL BODY.

Given the amount of pain she had in her face and behind her right eye on Thanksgiving and over the weekend, our main focus is keeping the pain under control.

Damn ugly forsaken disease.

There is absolutely nothing I can do to stop this or slow it down. My mother is going to die. Period. End of story.

It is not fair.

My religion tells me this is not the end of the story at all, but rather the beginning of eternal life.

But I am entitled to feel sad, depressed, lonely, empty.

She is not dead yet, but I really miss my mom.

My

M
O
M.

CHAPTER FIFTEEN

The Day

G. Arlene Cable
May 10, 1943 - December 6, 2003

When the phone rang that morning I knew this leg of our journey had finally ended.

Through her tears Patty was able to say in a slightly quivering voice, "Mom left us this morning."

"Oh, Patty!" I heard myself saying, bursting with emotion.

How could my very empty chest feel so heavy?

I was sorrowful yet relieved.

My rational side took over for a minute, realizing I was about thirty minutes away, in my PJ's and eager to get there quickly for a final goodbye.

"Okay, Patty. I'll be there as soon as I can. Did you call Suzie? Kathy? How's Dad? Did you call Hospice?"

It was the shortest phone conversation my sister and I had in months. There had been so much to discuss regarding mom's care, her condition, medications, regression, nurses' visits, etc.

No need for all that now.

My husband got up and put the coffee on as I tried to get myself dressed. This otherwise simple task became a series of decisions to make. I pulled different sweatshirts from the dresser. White socks or colorful socks today...*stop this silliness,* I told myself, realizing I was subconsciously stalling. I knew once I got there and said goodbye to my mother's now corpse, they would eventually take her away. We would have the services, and I would have to transition myself back into the normal routine of work, home, social life, a daily life without my mom. Until the last month or two I talked to my mom every day for as long as I can remember. Except maybe when I was away at college and I was a little too "cool" for her.

Through it all, Al has been nothing but supportive. He insisted on driving me to my parents' house, even though he was scheduled to referee the local basketball games that morning. I tried to convince him to meet me there later; it was silly for him to drive back and forth. As the doting husband whose wife just lost her mother, he would not have it. Plus I knew and respected how close he and mom had become. He wanted to say goodbye as well. He has been in my life for just about as long as the return of the "disease" invaded our family. He has journeyed this with us. The statistics said mom would live for about two years with the cancer in her bones. She lived four. Ha.

In spite of my challenges with dressing that December morning, I managed to tie my shoes, and we were out the door by 7:00 a.m. Al sped down our little dead-end street.

"Now, honey," I said, "no need to rush. Hospice is in no rush to, well, have her, I mean take her...we can have as much time as we need with her, plus Suzie is over an hour away, and I'm sure she wants to get there, too."

"Okay, hon, I know, I know."

"You know, Al, I feel so calm, really. I'm okay. I'm gonna be okay."

"I know, babe," he said as he put a comforting hand on my leg.

I knew I had to call a co-worker to cover for me. As a leasing agent at the time, Saturday had been the only day I was working. How nice of mom to die on a Saturday, excusing me of my duties. I know I used the cell phone to make the call, but it is strange...I cannot remember it now. I do not remember the rest of the drive, either.

I saw my father first. The sorrow in his expression told his story. He greeted me in the kitchen and embraced me. We burst into tears. We hugged and cried like that for a couple of minutes. He said how glad he was that mom was not suffering anymore, and what a good life they had.

When I look back to all of those days my dad greeted me by the back door, I barely had time to kiss him on the cheek as I dropped my purse and tote bag on the table en route to check on mom. Suddenly I had all the time in the world.

My niece Karlie greeted me in the hallway. This started another session of hugging and crying. At first she was consoling me. And then I felt her chest move heavily with each deep, heart-wrenching sob. We held each other like that for a long time. And Karlie sobbed. Losing her grandma was going to be one of those painful life lessons. The relationship between a grandmother and granddaughter is so completely unconditional.

All at once, while holding her, I thought of my own grandma's death. I thought of Karlie going through this process, knowing full well when she came out on the other side she would be just fine. She will follow in the footsteps of the wonderful women who have preceded her in our family.

I caught a glimpse of the hospice nurse, Janine, and my brain processed her gentle voice yet I could not comprehend any conversation.

It was time for me to go into the living room and see with my own two eyes that my mom was finally at rest. I rounded the corner into the living room.

There was no irregular breathing, no rattling. No urgency to check mom's medication log and assess if she needed more resting medicine, more morphine. No groaning, no struggling, no pain. No tremors, no sweating, no more cold feet.

Sorry, CANCER – this ride is over…my mom went to HEAVEN and left you behind to rot.

UGLY DISEASE
I HATE YOU

Now I focused on my peaceful mother, well not really my mother, just the cute four foot eleven inch vehicle ("I'm five feet with shoes!" she would say), the body which carried her spirit for sixty years. The person we all would recognize in a photograph or at the supermarket as "Arlene Cable."

My mom loved her two faithful little dogs, one black and one white. The black Pekinese mix, Silkie, sat near the bedside. She was obviously out of sorts and looked expectantly at all of us. The other dog, a fluffy white bichon named Mitzi, lay tight against my mother's leg. She was sprawled on her belly with her chin on her paws. It was the first time she did not go nuts when I came through the door. Mom had Mitzi when I used to live at home; so Mitzi loved it when I came to visit. She was too depressed to even lift her head. Mitzi missed her mama, too. Later my father would tell me that these little dogs actually howled when "it" happened. They had never howled before.

My mother's eyes were closed; she was asleep forever. I thought I felt fine, perhaps numb, and then all of a sudden I could no longer contain an overflowing well from the junkyard. I leaned over and brushed my face against her soft cheek. Her smell was so familiar, so "mom." I took it all in.

I buried my face in her soft blanket and cried out, "Oh, Mom! I'm so glad for you! THANK YOU!" I got louder still...sobbing uncontrollably. I was literally *shouting*: "I'm glad, Mom! I'M GLAD FOR YOU! THANK YOU! I LOVE YOU!"

I somehow managed to straighten myself and turned to find my husband, my rock, as he steadied me and held me close and wiped my tears. I hugged Janine. I hugged Patty. I hugged Karlie again. I hugged my brother-in-law, Pat.

Now all I had to do was figure out how I would live the rest of my days on earth without my mother.

CHAPTER SIXTEEN

Visitation Day

December 10, 2003

It did not bother me one bit to see her. She looked beautiful. She looked like mom sleeping, like the old mom we knew, not the sick mom. The sick mom never rested that peacefully anymore.

At our request, based on the fact that mom wore no makeup on a daily basis, they went "light on the cosmetics," as the funeral director put it. They chose a pretty, soft pink for her lips just to make her look natural.

Mom was always beautiful in blue and would have been proud. She wore the same dress she wore to my wedding just five months ago. In fact, when we shopped for it, we both agreed the dress would serve nicely for both occasions.

What a wonderful day my wedding had been. And she danced! And she smiled! And she spent time with so many family members and friends who had traveled from different parts of the country. She enjoyed the company of her beloved aunt, who traveled over five hundred miles to see her. My mother was often so happy in spite of her illness. She is an example to us all.

I picture her spirit now, happy and free, with God and the ones who have gone before. I can hear her laugh. Her mannerisms...her smile...her blue eyes crinkling at the corners...so much of her is forever stamped in my memory. She gave us everything that was meant to be. All of the life lessons, conversations, laughter, memories, etc. that I will need...it is all right here in the junkyard now. C'mon, we all know that you can find many useful things at a junkyard; sometimes to find it you just have to sort through the dirty junk first.

She is free of that heavy failing body.

The lasting impression of her life is permanently embedded deep within my heart. *Within the hearts of many.*

If I could say anything to her right now I would say,

"THANK YOU! KUDOS TO A GREAT LIFE, LADY!"

I can feel the spirit of my mother inside me. We all have someone like this in our lives. It does not necessarily have to be your own mother. Maybe you never knew your mother. Maybe you never liked your own mother. But God gave you *someone* who believed in you and loved you unconditionally, and you are a better person, a healthier *you* because that person loved you and guided you. What a gift! Now go and give the gift to others and feel the love of Jesus transcend you!

We had assembled five picture boards to tell the story of Arlene Cable's life. We wanted to personalize her wake, really celebrate her life. In the days before the services, we gathered up the picture boards we had so carefully prepared and brought them to the funeral home. In addition we brought a couple of her stamp collection books, including birds and elephants.

Instead of a flower spray (mom was not a big fan of fresh flowers...first of all she was allergic to them, and second of all she said they reminded her of a funeral...go figure), we decided it would be appropriate to drape the last quilt she made over her casket. We placed another one of her quilts over the couch where the family sits. We displayed needlepoint projects and the ribbons she won at the DuPage County Fair.

I absolutely loved it when people told me how much I resemble her high school pictures. I am sure my sisters felt the same way. It gave me a much needed sense of belonging; so often while growing up I dealt with my issues of being different. I was different. I was the only one with bright red hair and the fair skin to go with it. Since my mother's childhood pictures are black and white, you can see past the difference in our complexions and appreciate the resemblance in our faces. Truthfully, though, Patty is the one who really looks like her, along with Suzie's oldest daughter, Adrianna. Yes, my mother's legacy lives on. Her legacy lives on in all of those touched by her grace.

I feel I have a long way to go, a lot more learning to do. Maybe this experience is sort of the beginning of my whole story, and I need it to walk the path ahead.

It is so liberating to be an adult and finally appreciate the woman in your mother. What a beautiful, wonderful, strong, caring, smart, funny, wholesome person she was. I will always admire her ability to work with special needs children and adults. She cared for them as much as she cared for us and many times acted as an advocate. She did not care what her co-workers thought if she believed she could better the life of a child who could not speak for him or herself.

I have experienced so much "anticipatory grief." I learned that is what you call it when you know someone is going to die. I wanted to leave my own grief in the junkyard and share the good things about my mom yesterday at the wake. I saw people whom I either had not seen for years or whom I had never met before. I found great comfort in the stories that my mother's former co-workers shared. These conversations helped me to complete and fill in the memory of my mother, the teacher, the caregiver. One co-worker was very cheerful in relaying stories about mom. She told me if we girls have our mother's spirit, then we are lucky. And I do feel lucky.

At my mother's wake I spoke briefly with Nan, the hospice chaplain who came to know mom during the end of her life. Mom often requested to see her. I found myself relaying what a wonderful experience this has been, to be able to take care of my mother. I told her I realized it was a learning experience, and I would not trade it for anything, no matter how difficult the journey had been.

To my surprise Nan suggested I write some of my thoughts down. I told her I had in fact been journaling all along. She asked if I would share my notes with her. I said I would. She looked me in the eye and with a slight grin said, "Promise?"

I hesitated and glanced at my sleeping mother. I am not one to make promises unless I mean it, especially to people I hardly know.

"I promise."

Perhaps writing and sharing my thoughts about all this is a little self-serving. Perhaps I feel if I can share it then it is not all in vain.

I hardly cried at the visitation. I just cried at the end, when I had to leave her there that evening. I suppose I did not want it to be over. A funeral is so FINAL. I knew that was the next step. *But then what?*

• ❦ •

We will bury my mom today December 11, 2003

The funeral is simply too painful to write about. I remember bits and pieces, but I choose not to relive this day. You just have to somehow get through it. Aunt Sheila played the hymns my mother chose on the organ. Uncle Jack gave a sermon and said some funny things and some wonderful things about his little sister. Friends and former co-workers got up and spoke. Al surprised me when he got up to say a few words. This is when I learned he lay in bed with my mother one day and shared some final important thoughts with her.

We held the funeral luncheon at the same place where we enjoyed our wedding reception just five months earlier. I remember Al's brother Mick brought my dad an extra piece of chicken instead of dessert, and we all thought that was very funny. Leave it to Mick for a good laugh. Yes, I am part of the Keilman family now.

I think I am numb. I have no idea how to live without my mom. Taking care of her occupied so much of me, my time and my energy...*now what do I do?*

CHAPTER SEVENTEEN

Elephants

December 15, 2003

We like to travel to Lake Geneva, Wisconsin for overnighters with our best friends, Annie and Joe. Sometimes we take their three kids with us, and sometimes we don't. Annie mentioned a few months ago that they were planning a mid-December night away to enjoy the holiday scenery up there with the kids. We both knew that because of my mom's condition, Al and I would have to take a pass this year. A day or two after the funeral, Al asked me if I wanted to go.

"Honey, do you want to see if I can get a room at the Cove?" he asked.

"I don't know, Al. I'm not really in the mood for anything. I don't feel like going and pretending as if I am having a good time."

"It's just Joe and Annie, Mare. You don't have to put on any airs. I think you need to get away," he said as he reached for the phone.

He called the Cove and mentioned our friends' last name and told them he wanted a room right next to theirs if possible. It was done. On December 15th as we drove away from our town I felt liberated and sad all at the same time. I was thankful that Al was with me, whisking me away from my familiar, grief-stricken environment. I could not wait to see the look on Annie's face when I knocked on her hotel door. I felt like we were on a mission. It was a mission to run away from the junkyard, even if just for a day or two. Everything in my normal environment was one big painful reminder of my mother's permanent absence.

I think there is only so much pain your brain and your body can process. I was on overload and coming down from my long journey through the dying process.

My best friend Annie is the all-American girl. She is beautiful, inside and out. She has green eyes and blonde hair and a perfectly contagious smile. What makes her even more appealing is the fact that she has no idea how pretty she is. Her husband Joe and Al work together, and we all get along really well.

When we arrived that evening, Annie greeted us at her door, just as I had pictured. I figured if we did not find them in their room we would find them at the indoor pool with the kids.

"Hi, Sweetie!" she said as she wrapped her arms around me. "I'm so glad you came." She stepped back and took a good look into my eyes, still holding onto my arms. "Are you okay?"

The sincere concern and affection in her sweet voice pulled a heart string. I could not answer. Annie read my mind; I did not have to answer out loud. She knew I was as okay as I could be considering my mom died nine days ago. I just nodded. She nodded back at me with that Annie sort of understanding in her eyes. "Oh, Mare," she said as she hugged me one more time. By then the kids were pushing past their mother to hug me and Al, too.

I distracted myself from my sorrows as we played with the kids at the pool. Afterwards Annie, the kids, and I changed into our PJ's, hung out, and ate junk food. The guys went out for a couple of hours so we could talk. Annie has a big heart and has been so sympathetic to me through all of this. Her heart breaks for me, too.

I give Annie (and ALL of my friends) a lot of credit for putting up with me during this very painful time. I cried on her many times. I am sure there were times when she felt at a loss for words as I dumped some of my grief on her. Now that is a sign of a true friend – someone who will carry part of your junk when your junkyard is so full you cannot help but let it overflow into theirs. Not to mention this experience has unleashed a morbid side of my sense of humor that often pushes Annie's comfort level to the limit. I think nothing of making jokes about death and dying. Perhaps it is part of my defense mechanism, a way to make something very heavy seem light for a minute.

"I can't understand how you can joke like that about your mom..." she will say as she sighs and shakes her head.

"Well, Annie, we are all going to die. That's the promise, isn't it?"

"I know, Mare, but I cannot imagine losing my mom, let alone make jokes about it!"

"Annie, when that time comes you will be just fine. God will make sure you get everything you need from her before that happens."

I awoke early the following morning and quietly slipped out of bed so as not to wake my husband. We had our usual suite at the Cove, so I padded into the kitchen and put a pot of coffee on. It was only 5:30 a.m. but I could not sleep. My body was not yet used to regular sleep. I found an extra blanket in the closet and curled up with it on the couch as I sipped my coffee.

I was still getting used to being "free." I had taken the rest of December off from work, and I had no set plans. At a time when everything else in the junkyard seemed broken, this lack of schedule was a relief. I sat and reflected on what my family and I had been through. I realized the only reason I was here was because my mom no longer needed me. Damn, that hurts.

One consolation was that I had helped Patty bathe our mother the day before she died. We had been really good about respecting her and keeping her very clean and comfortable. As the funeral director and his assistant took our mother's corpse away, Patty and I agreed she would have been proud to know she went out "clean."

I put the television on very low. As I flipped through the channels I came across an infomercial with a guy talking. Just the guy; he was all that occupied the screen besides a picture hanging on the wall in the background. I noticed it because it was a drawing of an elephant. I inherited my mother's love of elephants, and we both enjoyed collecting them. Often I would buy her one for her birthday or for Christmas.

"Oh, Mary! Where did you find this? I don't have one like this!" she would say with delight as she unwrapped the elephant treasure I had found.

I flipped up one station. There was a commercial advertising a documentary about elephants in Africa. I watched with affection as a mama elephant interacted with her calf. I flipped up one more. There was a cartoon of a little boy pulling with all of his might on a leash. As he pulled, the animal on the other end of the leash came walking across the screen - it was an elephant. I flipped again, and again, and again, and again. Seven channels *in a row* showed me an elephant in one form or another. The hairs on the back of my neck stood up as a chill rushed over my body.

Some people call it coincidence. I call it my guardian angel.

CHAPTER EIGHTEEN

Mom's Birthday and Father's Day: One Up Day, One Down Day

It is May 10, 2004. My mother would have turned sixty-one today. Her birthday often fell on Mother's Day. I do not recall writing it, but in my handwriting I see a note on my calendar that says, "Mom would want you to be happy!"

And my note to myself worked. I have been terribly depressed on and off through the grieving...but I am not going to decide to be depressed on her birthday, on the holidays, etc. If I feel sad, fine...but if I do not, even better. I do not want to decide now to be sad on my mother's birthday twenty years from now. If I am sad, great, I am entitled to be sad; after all, my mom died. But my mom wants me to be happy.

Think about it. For sixty years my mother *celebrated* her birthday. Why, for the next sixty or so years of my life, would I choose to be sad on May 10th?

• • •

Father's Day 2004

Last Sunday was Father's Day. Suzie, Kathy, and I took our dad out to enjoy one of his favorite things. Eat. Husbands and little nieces were along, too. It was fun. Patty was away on vacation.

Afterward, since we were all together, we decided we should go through some more of mom's stuff. We four sisters had already sorted through and distributed the majority of it. Suzie and I had gone through my mom's closet and dresser drawers and thoroughly cleaned them out. What a painful process. I kept a few pairs of her cute little socks. I even kept an ugly pair, just because they have elephants on them, which I will never wear. Eventually they will rotate to the bottom of my already overflowing sock drawer to be forgotten. The experts call stuff like that "memory clutter."

On the day my sisters and I went through the majority of my mom's "stuff," we were at it for hours, sorting through jewelry, old glassware, collectibles, Beanie Babies, elephants, paper weights, hens on a nest...

Several months before mom died, I wrote down her final instructions as she dictated them to me. It was several pages typed. This was a way for her to maintain control of something in her life when she could not control the disease.

"As you go through my things and find something you might like to have, love one another and be generous. You may get more pleasure from letting your sister have it."

Dad was in and out that day; we kept him busy by sending him to get more newspaper so we could wrap up all of our goodies. It is amazing what one person can accumulate in sixty years. Of course that someone was a pack rat who enjoyed all night flea markets.

The best revelation I had after I got to keep some of my mom's "stuff" was I realized how much she enjoyed her "stuff." Now she is in a place where she does not need to be burdened with all this "stuff," and therefore will not have to worry about ever dusting this "stuff" again. My sisters and I can enjoy and dust the remainders of her "stuff," and someday my nieces will get to keep and enjoy and dust hopefully even less of this same "stuff."

I should add that in spite of my lack of interest in stamp collecting, I could not part with all of the extra bird stamps and stamp collecting supplies. I brought home small plastic tubs full and promptly stored them in the basement to be forgotten. I thought maybe I could put them together in little books for my nieces as a remembrance of their grandma. I know I never will, but hey, it is the thought that counts, right? I just could not let this "stuff" go.

Anyway, there was not very much "stuff" left to sort through, probably a couple hours worth of work to do with odds and ends. I went into the spare bedroom, which we refer to as the "stamp room," as my mom stored tens of thousands of stamps here at one time. Yes, postage stamps, covers, old postcards. She donated most of it to a good friend to take what she wanted and give the rest to their philatelic club.

I peeked into the closet to find large plastic tubs filled with craft supplies...brand new needlepoint kits, etc. When my mom was still "with it" she had us pull some of this stuff out and encouraged the hospice staff to take whatever they wanted. And they did. It was nice.

I looked up and down at the bookshelf full of books. My sisters and I have all inherited our mother's love of reading. *I don't feel like going through this stuff,* I thought. I felt a little sick to my stomach. I felt sad and aggravated that here we are, and it is Father's Day, and my mom is dead. *I want my mom!*

I could hear the others cheerfully talking in another part of the house, the kitchen, or maybe the living room. I wandered down the hall and into the bedroom that my parents shared for years and years. When we were little they would lock themselves in and tell us to not disturb them because they had to "pay the bills." This was one of our favorite inside family jokes as we became adults.

This bedroom was my mother's favorite place to read. She would lie in bed and, by absorbing herself in a good book, could escape her busy life for a while. Many times she would stay up until the wee hours of the morning to knock off the last chapters of a juicy novel.

My father would say, "No, honey, you know I can sleep with the light on. You go right ahead. That doesn't bother me one bit."

He would lie close to her and kiss her and tell her he loved her. He would roll over and happily drift off to sleep.

Now,

he sleeps here...

alone.

Just then, as I stood in the bedroom, I found myself frozen in time with memories swirling all around me. I saw myself, my sisters, my parents at different ages. Although the memories were mostly happy ones, I did not feel happy. The painful reality took over and settled into the pit of my broken heart...again.

She is never coming back here. We will make no more memories with my mother. This place where I grew up will never be the same.

As I looked around the room my eyes focused on the lawyer's bookcase, once full and overflowing. Now it was empty save for the bottom two shelves. On the day we went through most of her things, we were in agreement, towards the end of that long day, that sorting through the contents of these two particular shelves posed a project for a different day, a fresh day. Now I stood there, very interested in the contents, yet hesitant, asking myself whether we should start here or in the stamp room. I slowly sat down on the bed. The others came in and found me in my mournful state. Suzie sat down next to me on the bed.

My father said, "Now, girls, if you're not up to this today, it is okay; you don't have to do it."

My father has said this to me before as I wandered from room to room before coming to the conclusion that I was not up to the task.

It hit me that Sunday, as I sat there with my family, my father insisting we do not have to go through this stuff...

I looked at my father. "But that's the problem, Dad. I won't *ever* feel like finishing this project. It's like admitting that she's really gone. She's dead and I miss her...*I miss her so much,*" I said with a partially fading voice as the tears came streaming down my face. I had that awful feeling you get in your chest when your feelings are hurt.

Grieving is so painful, emotionally and physically. It is like being very sick and there is no medication and you just have to let it run its course.

I cried and felt horrible for crying on Father's Day. My three-year-old niece, Isabelle (better known as Peanut) came in just then as I was blowing my nose. She saw my tears and looked me in the eye. Her big brown eyes grew bigger. I tried to look away.

"Why is Aunt Mary crying?" she asked her mother inquisitively.

"Aunt Mary is sad because Grandma died," Suzie said as she scooped up her little Peanut and held her in her lap.

Peanut looked at her mama and thought about that for a moment before looking at me. She extended her soft little hand and patted me on the arm. Through my tears I winked at her. My sweet father sat down at my other side and put a comforting arm around me.

I know why I felt the reluctance to finish those shelves. They contained old books and documents pertinent to our family history. Mom and I sorted through this stuff about four years ago when she knew her cancer was terminal. She wanted to make sure I understood the importance of it all, that some of the literature was written by my great-great-grandfather. It meant so much to her. Going through it now, without her guidance, and taking it out of this place, symbolized a certain finality.

I shoved my pain back in the junkyard and with a heavy heart managed to help my sisters work for a couple of hours that day, sorting through crafty stuff and books and whatever.

Later that evening I was so glad to get home to cry. I cried a lot. I cried hard. I cried in different rooms. I cried standing up. I cried sitting down. I blew my nose in front of the bathroom mirror and cried some more for the hurt in my expression. It was the kind of crying where you cry so hard you think it must all be out of you and then another wave comes along and you cry some more.

Allow yourself to cry.

My very wise husband left me alone to cry it out. There is a certain sort of crying that requires a hug and then you are all better. This was the *other* sort of crying. There was no escape from this; I may have been able to write my way through much of the dying process, but the grieving process...that is a different, painful, unwritten story.

As an outlet for my grief I would often sit and play songs on the piano which reminded me of my mother and made me cry. I not only needed to cry but I wanted to cry...I wanted to feel sad...I wanted to purge my pain although many times it seemed as if I would never feel better. If you are not already familiar with Willie Nelson's *Angel Flying Too Close to the Ground* listen to the words sometime. The story told in that song says so much; if it had meaning before I lost my mom, it has so much more meaning now. Songs like that take me back to riding in my parents' yellow Ford Maverick as my mom and dad sang along to the radio.

For a while after mom died I cried every day. Usually in the shower. But life goes on. You pick yourself up and you function somehow. You go to work, or wherever it is that you go, and you distract yourself with your life.

The hours pass,

and the days,

the months,

the years...

and slowly, ever so slowly, your broken heart mends so you do not have to cry every day...

because your mom died.

CHAPTER NINETEEN

The Dream

Thursday in late June 2004
4:01 a.m.

It is an amazing experience to dream of someone who has passed. I have to write this now as I am afraid if I go back to sleep I will forget the details of dreaming about my mother. You know how that is, when you wake up and you have dreamed of something, and you can see it in your mind, yet you cannot quite make sense of it with words.

She was sitting in her recliner. She looked "good"... her color was right. I could hear her voice exactly as it was when she was well. She had her glasses on. (She did not always wear her glasses toward the end.) And maybe a sweater? Or afghan...or maybe the animal blanket, the really soft one with the elephant and the giraffe on it that Margo made for her.

Anyway – unlike some dreams where the surroundings are surreal or dreamlike, this time we were in her living room, in the house where I grew up. It was the very place where she took her last breath just six months, two weeks, and four days ago.

"Mary, why do you think we are here?"

"We are here to love one another and touch one another."

"Yes," she said as she nodded her head in agreement. "Why else?"

"Um, I don't know, Mom. You tell me why we are here."

"We are here to help people recover. You helped me recover, and I feel good now."

"Wow, Mom."

"Some day I would like to help you recover, my little Mary."

I felt at peace.

Wow. Neat! I never thought of helping her die as comfortably as possible as helping her to "recover." Of course this makes sense to our religious side.

I am so thankful for this kind of dream. Right after she died I dreamed of her frequently, almost every night for a couple of weeks. Most of those dreams, however, were nightmares.

In one dream I found myself trying to care for her in a foreign hospital while juggling a new job. Everyone in the dream gave me direction in a language I did not understand, and then scoffed at me when I could not get anything right. The worst part about it was that my mother's illness was worsening because of my lack of understanding.

In another dream, I stood by her corpse in the back room of a funeral parlor. She appeared to take a breath. I concentrated, looked more closely, and nearly jumped out of my skin when she opened one eye and winked at me! In desperation I tried to convince those around me that she was alive. No one would believe me. I grew more desperate; but the funeral director calmly assured me such behavior on my mother's part was perfectly normal, and she was in fact dead...*dearly departed*, if you will.

Eventually the nightmares stopped.

My dream from last night was just the opposite. I feel wonderful and fulfilled. I can look at a hundred pictures of her...but to dream like this is a gift. Wow. I wish this for everyone. I heard her voice! I saw her familiar mannerisms...a certain pause and tilt of her head as she contemplated her words of wisdom or comfort. Oh, it is wonderful and certainly worth getting up at 4:01 a.m. to write about.

CHAPTER TWENTY

Just Write It

March 29, 2007

I should be working out, which has become part of my regular morning routine over the past fourteen months. But today, I will start my day by writing.

About a year and a half after my mom's passing, I changed jobs and now manage an apartment building for people fifty-five and older. When residents are not home, their packages are delivered to my office. One of my ladies called the office recently to see if there was a package for her. There was.

"I want you to open it," she said.

Half out loud I thought, "Huh?"

"Go ahead, open it!" she said.

"Okay."

What I discovered inside was a book...and *her* name as the author. This led to a conversation about getting a book published; I expressed some interest.

Yesterday my resident-author, Leanne, stopped by the office. She was so kind to share her experience about getting published, and encouraged me to move forward with my book.

So much has happened in my life. I changed jobs and lost twenty-five of the pounds I gained as I ate my way through my grieving.

Over a year ago on New Year's Day 2006 I sat on the couch, feeling fat and sluggish, blaming it all on the death of my too-young mother. *Wait a second,* I told myself; *it had been over two years since she passed.* Maybe it was time to stop blaming every bad thing in my junkyard on my mom's cancer.

Two years is long enough, I told myself. *I am going to get myself back.* It was almost as if someone had flipped a switch.

I got off the couch, squeezed into some spandex shorts that I bought several pounds ago, and went for a workout in my basement. I started with a whopping eighteen minute, one mile workout tape. As the months passed I graduated to the two mile, and then the three mile, and then to even more advanced workout tapes. All in the comfort of my own basement. You know what? The pounds just started melting off.

I *allowed* myself to realize it was okay to be happy again. I *allowed* myself to shed some of that weight, the protective wall I had built up around myself while my mom was dying. I did not need that wall anymore. I was really getting better.

I have lost the weight slowly, and that is fine with me. If I lose twenty more I will be at the size I want to be. But I still love myself *now*, just the way I am. I have found you have to love yourself *first* in order to make the lifestyle changes that will allow you to be healthy, mentally and physically, for the long term. I used to think that losing ten or twenty pounds was the magic key to true self happiness. We women are so very critical of ourselves; let's just all stop it. Life is too short!

As Leanne sat across from me, the passion for *doing* something with my book all came rushing back. I have always felt the passion to write a book; what am I waiting for?

That evening I told Al all about Leanne and our conversation about writing, etc. This was not the first time I expressed my passion to share my experiences. He looked at me with those blue eyes I fell in love with. With great sincerity in his voice he said, "You just have to do it. I'm behind you all the way."

But this is all so personal, I tell myself.

My would-be book floats around the house in different places...on the kitchen counter with a stack of magazines that I will never make the time to read....or in a drawer to be forgotten until I need to retrieve something there. I found this passage among my notes from about a year ago:

I am working on my book. It has been over two years since my mom died and I am typing this and editing it as I go and trying not to cry the whole way through it. That is why I have not found the courage to pursue this until now, because as I write I emotionally experience things all over again. It is exhausting. But I have felt the need, the desire from deep within to share this in hopes of helping others. There is a power within me, driving me.

The revelation. It hit me yesterday as I was discussing the "book" with my husband. *The junkyard.* When I re-read all of this and edit it and so forth, I must revisit the junkyard. I relive some of the most painful experiences of my life. My mom died. My mom died from cancer, and she suffered A LOT, and I saw it. *I saw it all.* When you watch a loved one suffer like that, and you help take care of them, and watch them dying, you forever lose some of the innocence which connected you with being your parent's child.

Many people go through this. I am not special.

All I know is I am a different and hopefully a better, more compassionate person because of it. Now when I hear of someone else going through this process, I feel a tinge of pain deep within my heart as I sympathize with their situation.

The pain of reliving my experiences has kept me from moving forward with my book; but it was always in the back of my mind. I felt an inner power, a force, a very raw need to do this. Now I can see that forcing myself to revisit this painful time helped me *finish* my grieving. I was finally able to purge some of the dark emotions that I had pushed way back in the deep corners of my junkyard. I dug in, got my hands dirty, and worked. I hurt, and I cried, and I worked some more.

Now that I have cleaned out some of the dirty junk, I have a lot more room for the good junk. I feel lighter. The pain will always remain; but I do not have to carry it around with me in my back pocket. I can store it in a corner of the yard and revisit it at appropriate times.

Three years and three months and twenty-three days later I still miss my mother, but...*I am going to be okay.*

CHAPTER TWENTY-ONE

The Healing Process

A little over a year after my mom passed away, I was feeling blue. I thought, *here comes Christmas number two without my mom.* (Insert sigh here.)

On Christmas Eve morning I forced myself out of the house. I went shopping for last minute specials. My mom and I loved to shop like that...just venture out and find little trinkets or treasures that reminded us of the little ones in the family, and giggle and say things like, "Oh, the girls will just love this, won't they?"

But now, here were the holidays again and after all, my mom was dead, so who cared if December ever came again? I put my melancholy self in the car anyway and started driving.

And you know what? I found the cutest little odds and ends at the local pharmacy. I thought to myself, "Oh, the girls will just love these," as I pictured their happy little faces. By forcing myself to get moving, I actually had fun. I rediscovered the Christmas spirit inside of me. I *found* some treasures and trinkets. I bought little extras for my sisters, my nieces. I vividly remember driving and thinking it would be a nice time to visit the cemetery on that brisk, sunny December day. I wanted to share this joy with my mom.

So I did.

Mom's grave is easy to find because not far from there stands a flag pole which proudly waves our glorious American flag.

I walked over to the grave, took a seat on the tombstone (this is when I realized how cold it really was), looked skyward, and had a little conversation with my mother.

I thanked her for all of the little shopping trips, the fun we had putting puzzles together, her wisdom, her sense of humor, all of it. I could see her in my mind. So many wonderful emotions, memories, you name it...it was all there at once. It was wonderful, powerful.

I realized just because she is not here anymore does not mean I cannot enjoy the things we used to do together.

I will repeat that.

I realized just because she is not here anymore does NOT mean I cannot enjoy the things we used to do together.

A year had passed. I was getting better. I will never stop missing her; however, the once very raw wounds on my heart and soul have almost healed. I decided it was time to let it go. I felt a physical release from my heart, my core. In spite of my cold butt, all at once I started laughing and crying and feeling thankful. I was so thankful I had this person in my life. The wind blew my red locks across my face as I wiped away my tears of sentiment.

When your heart breaks slowly for someone, you change. It takes a long long time for the heart to heal. Maybe it never heals completely. But the scar tissue which is formed during the healing process makes you who you are.

Use it.

Use your experiences to take your life up a notch.

Be in the moment.

Enjoy the people around you.

Be kind to a crabby person. Remember, you do not know what brought them to be crabby; maybe all they need is a little kindness and a smile or a helping hand.

Eat your favorite junk food without feeling guilty.

Be thankful for what you have.

Be kind to your spouse.

Stop judging people.

Love yourself, just the way you are. If you need a change, reach down and find the power within you to do it. You are in charge of yourself.

Treat yourself and others with respect.

Work hard. Do not stay at a job you do not like. If you do, do not use the fact that you dislike your job as an excuse to do a bad job. When you walk away each day, take pride in knowing you did your best for that day.

Ride your bicycle.

Go out and run around with your kids. If you do not have kids of your own, run around with someone else's.

Take care of your health.

Laugh every day.

Hug somebody.

Do not be so self-conscious about being too fat or too skinny.

Say "thank you" when someone gives you a compliment.

Compliment others.

Enjoy your loved ones RIGHT NOW, for one day you may miss them.

Be thankful for life's hardships...*God only gave them to you because your shoulders are big enough to carry them. With the hardships, allow your heart to grow. Know that some day, if you are lucky, the experience you have gained along your life path will allow you to help others.*

My parents raised me and loved me and gave me the tools to take care of myself. The thirty-one years that I spent with my mother were comprised of mostly happy things. That is a gift to be thankful for.

My mom died, and it had a great impact on my life...and I would not change a thing. It is all part of who I am now.

CHAPTER TWENTY-TWO

Do It Now

Sometimes it is healthy to interrupt your normal schedule in order to experience life's important events, especially the ones that will never come again. Recently I left work an hour early to see my ten-year-old niece's school play. It was downright inconvenient. This is a busy time at work, not to mention gas prices are through the roof. I drove an hour and a half to see Adrianna in a play which lasted just thirty minutes. BUT...as I entered the school with Suzie, Suzie's mother-in-law and my two other nieces, Adrianna saw me right away and came running down the hall. "Aunt Mary! Aunt Mary! Aunt Mary!" she yelled with excitement as she ran to me and gave me a great big hug. Well, that was all I needed...I forgot all about the price of gas. I spent those thirty minutes of the play laughing and beaming with pride as I realized how much practice and effort Adrianna and these kids put into it.

As we left the school and walked as a group back to the house, Suzie's middle daughter, Dianne, who is eight, stopped to adjust her flip flop. I stayed back with her, and then we raced to catch up to the group. I let her run ahead of me and then passed her, and then slowed down to let her get ahead again. All the while we were giggling and laughing at each other's silliness. Her sandal came off again and again, until finally she flipped it up in the air with her little foot, laughing and shrieking the whole time. Even at the age of thirty-five, my inner child still hangs around the junkyard once in awhile, and I thought that was pretty funny. I flipped my sandal up in the air, too.

We all went out to eat that evening. At their usual insistence to sit by Aunt Mary, I was squished between Dianne and Isabelle, now almost six, on a little bench seat of a booth at the local buffet in Mendota. I hardly ever get to see my nieces on a weeknight; in spite of spending half the evening making sure they kept their sticky fingers off of me, it was a real treat. By inconveniencing myself and busting out of my regular schedule, I cashed in on a memory. Was I tired on the long drive back? Yep, but I rolled the windows down, turned the radio up and sang the whole way home. Driving alone on long distances is somehow liberating and a great time to reflect on all of the good things in my life.

Thirty years from now no one will remember that I left work early; but my niece and I will remember that I was there to share in her fifth grade stardom.

So when it comes to living your life, DO IT NOW. For today we make the memories of tomorrow.

EPILOGUE

Poetry for the Soul

As a child I loved to learn. I was a *Sesame Street* kid all the way, and everyone in my family read to me...my mom, my dad, my sisters. I was constantly exposed to learning new words and new things. My mother told me one time as we were driving along, from my car seat I said, "Mommy, look at that garage door! It opened electronically." She peered at me in the rearview mirror and said, "Where did you learn the word 'electronically'?"

I think it was also from my car seat that I recited my first poem. My mom told me I shared it with her when I was barely old enough to talk.

"Mommy, I made up a poem!"

"Let's hear it," she encouraged me.

"Let's high
Let's high
Let's up in the sky...
And truly amble slow"

We repeated it to each other many times over the years. I would shout it out to her now...*if only she could hear me...*

• ♡ •

Will I Find You, Grandma?

I have kept this poem in a drawer for about ten years. When I first wrote it I shared it with a few of my relatives, and if I remember correctly, I made my Uncle Jack cry over the phone (although of course that was not my intention). I wrote it after the sudden death of my mother's mother, my grandma, who passed away of natural causes at the age of seventy-five. Although we were separated by more than five hundred miles, our souls were connected. From the time I learned to write I remember corresponding with her, and our letter writing continued through my college years and into adulthood. She never opened the last letter I sent; it arrived the day after she died.

A few months after she passed, I found myself having one of those days. If you have ever grieved for someone, you know what those moments of desperation feel like. I had that awful heavy painful feeling of hopelessness in my chest. I sat at the kitchen table and just started writing. I wrote down all of the things my memory had in store about my grandma. All of the things she taught me. All of the connections we had. Everything about her. And I cried...a lot. Little did I know that as I wrote, and as I cried, I was purging some of the pain that is associated with grieving. Even less did I know that this writing habit would some day help to bring me through the grieving for my own mother.

For me, it is writing. For you, it may be something else. Follow your instincts when you are going through something tough in your life, and you will figure out what your healthy outlet is. Maybe it is watching your favorite sad movie, the one which makes you cry every time you watch it. (*Terms of Endearment* does it for me...or *Titanic.*) Maybe it is going for a long walk so you can sort through your thoughts. You know what it is. God gave us the grieving process, but he also gave us the ability to heal.

The bottom line is that our loved ones who have passed would not want us to go on grieving indefinitely. By all means, you HAVE to go through the grieving process. With time I have *accepted* that life is *different* now. Do I still cry over my mom? Sure I do. But mostly her memory brings joy and happiness.

Now *my* job is to share what she gave me with others.

Here is the poem which I constructed from all of my notes the day I could not stop crying about the loss of my grandma.

January 15, 1997
Will I Find You, Grandma?

Sit down with me, Grandma. Let's have some coffee. You can put breakfast on the table as we discuss how to spend the day.
Will I find you when all of our plans are made?

Sit with me on the porch swing, Grandma. Let's chat awhile. Tell me the latest about your neighbor Lizzie as we look over the Stony Creek.
Will I find you if I go down to the water?

Sit down with me in the living room, Grandma. Let's watch TV. "Days" is about to start and you can explain what's going on.
Will I find you when the program is over?

Sit down with me in the kitchen, Grandma. Let's have some lunch. No, I do not mind eating at eleven o'clock. We will clean up together when we're done.
Maybe I'll find you amongst the dishes.

Sit down with me at the table, Grandma. Let's play canasta. I want to hear you giggle when you beat me.

Will I find you in this deck of cards?

Sit down with me, Grandma. Let's read awhile. Is that book any good? You must have read this one already; your initials are in it.

Will I find you when the last page is turned?

Sit down with me at the card table, Grandma. Let's put a puzzle together. Oh yes, that one is pretty.

Do you think I'll find you when all the pieces are together?

Sit down with me at my house, Grandma. Let's quilt awhile. Remember when I was about twelve, and you helped me piece my first quilt?

I wonder if I'll find you when the last stitch is sewn.

Lie down with me now, Grandma. Let's go to bed. We'll talk for awhile. I'll assure you that you bought enough food for all those people coming to dinner tomorrow.

We'll talk about my dad and tell the chicken story... about the time he wanted the last piece but you had "plans" for it. When we giggle, someone in a different part of the house will tell us to be quiet and go to sleep. Of course this will make us laugh even more.

If you cannot sleep right away you'll take an aspirin or get a Rolaids from your top dresser drawer. You'll offer one to me, too.

Then I'll give you an update on your great-grandchildren, my nieces and nephews. You'll tell me a story about your beloved Ernie, and I'll miss a grandpa I never knew.

We'll talk about Uncle David and then lie there in silence for a minute or two, missing him. We will agree that Aunt Kathy will always be family to us, even though her new family has grown.

And if I am cold, you'll get right up and pull a blanket out of the cedar chest and cover me up. Five minutes later when I am drifting off to sleep, you'll wake me up to ask if I am warm enough.

So, Grandma, if I fall asleep, will I find you in my dreams?

You are not in the kitchen, or in the living room, or on the front porch. When I put a puzzle together, all the pieces go in, but there is still something missing.

When I finish a good book, I do not feel finished. I want to read on. I want to find you there.

And yet I continue to play cards and quilt and read and put puzzles together and all that stuff. Because some day when it does not hurt anymore, when I do not miss you every day...

I will find you there amongst the puzzles and the books.

Grandma, I will find you there again.

Printed in the United States
86299LV00003B/169-300/A